IMAGES
of America

LOST RESORTS
OF THE
IOWA GREAT LAKES

ON THE COVER: From 1949 until today, this beach at Vacation Village has attracted playful sun worshippers all summer long. Vacation Village was created with families in mind, with small cottages for sleeping, a dining hall, and even an activities director. It is now a timeshare resort known as Village West. (Courtesy of Carl and Nancy Ross.)

IMAGES
of America

LOST RESORTS
OF THE
IOWA GREAT LAKES

Jonathan M. Reed

ARCADIA
PUBLISHING

Copyright © 2020 by Jonathan M. Reed
ISBN 978-1-4671-0320-6

Published by Arcadia Publishing
Charleston, South Carolina

Printed in the United States of America

Library of Congress Control Number: 2018960157

For all general information, please contact Arcadia Publishing:
Telephone 843-853-2070
Fax 843-853-0044
E-mail sales@arcadiapublishing.com
For customer service and orders:
Toll-Free 1-888-313-2665

Visit us on the Internet at www.arcadiapublishing.com

This book is dedicated to all the memories created at the Iowa Great Lakes. May future generations enjoy these lakes as much as we did.

CONTENTS

ACKNOWLEDGMENTS

When I completed *Okoboji and the Iowa Great Lakes*, there was no intention to embark on another book. Then, the Inn of Okoboji was put up for auction and sold. Public reaction was mute, unlike during the 1999 Save the Park campaign, which was a successful effort to buy and preserve the Arnolds Park Amusement Park. The once-grand Inn would slide into history with no fanfare, joining dozens of other Iowa Great Lakes resorts that now exist only in memories.

Thanks go out to several people and organizations that contributed to the research effort. First is Mary Kennedy, curator of the Iowa Great Lakes Maritime Museum, and her late husband, Steve Kennedy, who gathered the many historical images. Mary has been a constant friend and supporter of these efforts as well as a dandy proofreader and fact-checker.

The Dickinson County Historical Museum in Spirit Lake is a gem that every area vacationer should visit. Cindy Schubert and others there were exceedingly helpful in chasing down images and facts. Another museum that should not be missed is the Higgins Museum of National Bank Notes in Okoboji. In addition to presenting banking history, founder William R. Higgins Jr. amassed a broad and well-organized postcard collection representing every county in Iowa. Thanks go to Larry Adams, the curator.

Once again, I must acknowledge my friend R. Aubrey LaFoy, local historian, columnist, prolific author, and all-around great guy. Thanks to his 90-plus years, he directly remembers more about the area than anyone you will ever meet—a true testament to paying attention. May I be able to greet you and shake your hand for years to come, Aubrey.

Preservation Advantage Companies, which maintains the newspaper archives of Dickinson County (and others) and the Spirit Lake Library, also deserves thanks, inasmuch as nothing would have gotten done without their valuable services.

Finally, thanks must be given to all those who came forward with photographs from family scrapbooks, flyers from drawers, and recollections of summer vacations from decades long past. Unless otherwise noted, all photographs appear courtesy of the Iowa Great Lakes Maritime Museum.

INTRODUCTION

For generations of families, the pure, clean water of Okoboji and the Iowa Great Lakes in northwest Iowa has been a cherished vacation destination. Also for decades, large resorts and dozens of mom-and-pop cabins welcomed these vacationers year after year. Many times, resort operators would watch children grow up and return with their own families. However, only a few of these resorts survive today.

Abundant wildlife drew hunters and fishermen beginning in the late 1860s. Ducks, geese, pheasant, prairie chicken, and seemingly unlimited quantities of fish were the primary attractions, and locals were quick to welcome sportsmen. Rooming houses and hotels in the town of Spirit Lake popped up, with Billy Lillywhite building the Lillywhite Lodge on the west side of Spirit Lake on the stage line route. In 1871, pioneer Orlando Crandall built the modest Hunter's Lodge on Spirit Lake's northwest shore. Upon its immediate success, Crandall improved the property, turning it into the much larger Crandall's Lodge. One mile to the east, W.D. Sampson established Sampson's Lodge on McClelland's Beach. In the 1870s and early 1880s, Big Spirit became the focus for vacationers.

These successes impelled the Burlington, Cedar Rapids and Northern Railway (BCR&N) of Cedar Rapids, Iowa, to push through service to Spirit Lake, which it did in 1882. The following year, the railroad constructed the grandest, most magnificent hotel ever built here, the Hotel Orleans. This boasted all that the wealthy from Chicago, Omaha, or St. Louis could desire: comfortable and airy rooms with indoor plumbing, spectacular views of the prairie and lakes, a bowling alley, laundry, telegraph service, and fine dining.

At this time, a Des Moines businessman named D.B. Lyon saw an opportunity and bought hundreds of acres on the west side of West Okoboji. His resort, Manhattan, began with a simple bathhouse and accommodations but almost immediately expanded in hopes of overcoming poor access. Roads were limited on that side of the lake, it was too far from rail stations, and guests had to chiefly rely on the resort's steamship. Manhattan went bust in 1899, but subsequent owners continued to expand and adapt to the times for more than three decades. Survival during this period was enabled by selling off lots and excess acres to create cash flow.

West Okoboji's greatest resort was the Inn. Begun in the late 1890s and enlarged for three consecutive years, it quickly became the financial success that eluded Manhattan's owners. Developer J.A. Beck chose a far better location—directly in front of Okoboji's deepest water—that cooled guests. Visitors arriving by train at the Okoboji station could catch a hack (carriage) to the Inn while their luggage would follow behind—no steamship ride necessary. In 1903, Beck turned over management of the Inn to two sisters who were fondly known around the area as Aunt Polly and Aunt Sarah. Under their four decades of guidance, the Inn became the preferred vacation destination around the lakes. After World War II, the Inn's new owners recognized that the old buildings were seen as threadbare, shabby, and run-down; they were demolished in 1955. Locals heralded the construction of the modern New Inn in 1957, which offered comfortable motel-style accommodation, air conditioning, and a swimming pool.

As customers evolved from solo sportsmen to wealthy couples to families, so did guests' expectations of an Okoboji vacation. One of the last owners of the original Manhattan resort, for instance, had the drafty facility torn down in the 1930s and used the lumber to build tidy guest cabins. A few years later, he bought lakefront farmland to the north and created the purpose-built Vacation Village, a resort offering family-oriented activities that resonated with post–World War II vacationers—and their children. Today, many of those visitors are bringing their grandchildren to Vacation Village's successor, Village West.

During all this time, the large resorts faced growing competition from small-time entrepreneurs for tourist dollars. Almost as soon as lakefront lots could be developed and sold, mom-and-pop resorts began to appear. Initially, many of these offered the bare essentials for a fishing vacation at Okoboji: a tiny cottage with a bed, perhaps a table and chair, and—if you were fortunate—a nearby outhouse. Meals were often eaten at the kitchen table in the host's residence. Dozens of these resorts sprang up around the Iowa Great Lakes bearing the owners' names. Former guests still hold fond memories of the resorts and their hosts. While there have been many over the years (it would be impractical to try to identify them all), a few of the names still widely recognized include Harlan Beach, Vestergaard's, Lee's Resort, Larson's Cottages, Brook's Beach, Gerk's, Babcock's Cottages, Clements Beach, Reed's Run, Lowcock Cottages, and Jimmy's Cottages. Others that are just as memorable include Lake View Beach, Oak Hill Cottages, the Villa, Jones Beach Cottages, Angler's Bay Resort, Camp Arrowhead, Camp Illini, and Camp Hiawatha. All are gone now. In fact, Big Spirit Lake has only a single traditional lakefront resort: Sandbar Beach.

The demise of the debt-burdened Inn on West Okoboji at the end of 2017 punctuated the changes evolving over time. Although it was once the norm among those with summer cottages at Okoboji, it is now rare that a family spends an entire summer here. Today, husband and wife often both work full-time, and lengthening school schedules compress the "summer vacation" to barely two months. Ever-increasing organized-sports obligations often mean that families grab a few weekends at the lake when they can instead of staying for the whole season.

The popularity of Okoboji as a vacation destination has, ironically, been the root cause of this change. As more and more people enjoyed the area, lakefront land values that began to rise in the 1970s positively skyrocketed in the 1990s. Increased property values also brought an increase in tax burdens. Older resort owners—who may have been struggling for years—reluctantly (or sometimes gratefully) began accepting offers by developers for their property. The quaint cabins and sleepy resorts have been replaced by large, modern private houses or condominiums, each with its own dock, boat hoist, and boat.

The cry that Okoboji has become a private playground for the wealthy is not without merit, at least based on lakefront property changes. Today, older million-dollar properties are routinely bulldozed for a house peculiar to the new owner's taste. This, in turn, has fostered growth, with more affordable off-lake condos and patio homes now being erected. These new accommodations are fundamentally changing the local economy as condo owners rent their vacation retreats to weekenders or full-week vacationers. The consequence of this is that the dollars that used to stay in the community from locally-owned resorts, regardless of size, now flow back to the home communities of the rental owners.

At the end of the day, though, Okoboji and the Iowa Great Lakes continue to be favored destinations in the upper Midwest. The grand resorts and quaint cottages may be gone, but the love of all that Okoboji has to offer still pulls people in.

One

Early Arrivals

The first accommodations for vacationers were around Big Spirit Lake. Englishman Billy Lillywhite and Orlando Crandall constructed buildings for guests in the early 1870s. Both of these buildings were stops on the stagecoach line between Spirit Lake and Jackson, Minnesota; rail service did not arrive at the Iowa Great Lakes until 1882. These early buildings were resorts in concept only and offered somewhat crude accommodations that only hunters, fishermen, and the occasional trapper would welcome. Slightly more refined was Sampson's Lodge on what is now McClelland's Beach. At this time, Big Spirit's water level was such that deep, sandy beaches existed for all to enjoy. Early photographs show practically the entire northwest shore of this lake with these beaches—and hardly a dock or building to intrude on solitude. It was this peace and quiet that attracted visitors, and it took almost no time for Crandall's simple hunting lodge to be enlarged and improved to eventually become Crandall's Lodge. Sampson's Lodge existed until about 1911. Lillywhite's hotel lasted, in various guises, until the 1930s. Crandall's Lodge, which was larger and better equipped to evolve with changing tastes, became a favorite of Big Spirit vacationers. It passed out of family hands after World War II and was sold and demolished in 1976. Today, Big Spirit Lake remains the "quiet lake" of the Iowa Great Lakes.

This building began it all. Hunter's Lodge was constructed by Orlando Crandall—believed to be the bearded man standing in the doorway—around 1871. This photograph likely documents the beginning of Crandall's dream to build a resort for hunters and fishermen on land he owned on the north shore of Spirit Lake. Although it was little more than a cabin with some beds, Crandall's Hunter's Lodge was nevertheless a success. An 1879 *Spirit Lake Beacon* newspaper clipping suggested the lodge was so busy that he had to hang guests in trees. Over the first few years, he built two additions to the lodge, which was eventually overshadowed by his much larger Crandall's Lodge. (Courtesy of the Dickinson County Historical Society.)

Quiet, stately, and shrewd businessman Orlando Crandall is shown here just a few years before he died in 1909. On his way west from Chenango County in New York State, Crandall had "traded nearly all his earthly possessions" to acquire land on the north shore of Big Spirit Lake from Rev. J.S. Prescott, a pioneer with a reputation for promoting questionable land dealings. When Crandall arrived in 1866 to inspect his property, he found Prescott had sold him "land" mostly beneath the surface of Big Spirit Lake. Structures or landmarks are evident today, but the 1883 map below shows the location of Crandall's Lodge, the Hunter's (Lodge) post office, and Sampson's Lodge, which was one mile to the east. At this time, Big Spirit Lake was virtually undeveloped, with deep sand beaches backing up to thick oak groves and swamps and sloughs farther north.

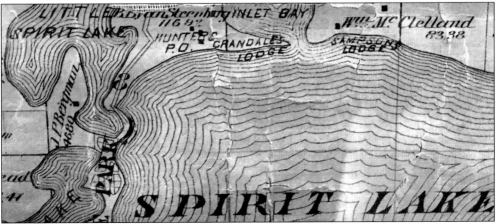

Orlando Crandall managed to acquire not just the Hunter's Lodge he helped construct but also adjacent property upon which he could build a proper resort hotel, which he did in 1879. This impressive structure with trendy Victorian bric-a-brac was easily identifiable and fashionable. Crandall's Lodge was said to mirror the comfort, convenience, and hospitality of his hotel in Spirit Lake, the Crandall House. Starting from when it opened, Crandall's Lodge was served by steamboats—a major advantage in days when access to areas around the lake was by trail. By 1900, Crandall's Lodge could comfortably accommodate more than 80 guests at once not only in the main building but in lakefront cabins, as well.

After arriving at Crandall's Lodge by steamboat, guests were greeted with a broad and deep sand beach, a sturdy dock, and the prospect of cool evenings on the wide porches. In the days before air conditioning, most rooms had windows that would allow breezes to come through. In these early years, summertime guests frequently occupied themselves with fishing, heading out on the water with a rowboat or sailboat, or bathing in Iowa's largest natural lake.

The sandy beaches afforded hijinks, too, as shown by this group of unidentified children photographed around 1930; one with a camera may have captured some of the images used in this book. However, these beaches would eventually become a rarity, because a series of dams built in Milford raised the level of all of the lakes to nearly the levels they are at today.

Crandall's Lodge, Spirit Lake, Ia.

On the Road to Crandalls

This postcard from the early 1900s shows that Crandall's Lodge was quite extensive, with wings and even a restaurant built for guests' enjoyment. The bottom of the postcard was no doubt meant to depict nature's beauty, which early vacationers would have welcomed. By this time, sailboats, steamers, and the occasional—but rare—powerboat could be found on Spirit Lake.

Highway 276   Phone 6-F2

CRANDALL'S LODGE

North Shore, Big Spirit Lake

COOL, QUIET PLACE TO SPEND
THE SUMMER

Home Cooking   **Marie Nefzger, Mgr.**

After Orlando Crandall died in 1909, operation of the lodge and the roughly 100 acres surrounding it was passed to his granddaughter, Marie Nefzger. She continued to welcome guests, help cook meals, and manage Crandall's Lodge for four decades. As was often the case around the Iowa Great Lakes area, resort operators began to either sell or lease land to generate annual income. Permanent cottages began to spring up on the Crandall property, although the land was leased.

Crandall's Lodge
Thomas Photo

Crandall's Lodge

In northern Iowa is a quaint old lodge filled with fond memories for me and other members of my family. This is Crandall's Lodge on Big Spirit Lake. The lodge is nearly one hundred years old. The rooms are furnished with authentic antique furniture, each room containing a wash stand, a porcelain basin, and pitcher.

In all the rooms a musty odor hangs, far different from the smoke-steeped smell of motel rooms. The dining room below the sleeping quarters is done in a rustic decor simply because it has never been changed. On the walls hang trophies of deer, elk, and other wild life, and pictures of some of the old owners of the lodge. The food is delicious! Much of it is grown in the large garden behind the kitchen, and all of it is homecooked — a far cry from the frozen, pre-cooked food found in many restaurants today. Extending around the front of the lodge on both floors is a porch where one can sit and meditate and look at the beautiful, misty lake. The legend of this lake says that an Indian princess fell in love with a common brave. But because he was not of royal blood, they could never hope to be wed with her father's blessing. They decided to run away together in a little birch bark canoe. They were seen as they tried to escape. But before her father and his braves could take chase, a storm came up, and they were never heard from again. The mist supposedly is their spirits rising from the water.

Although the paint is peeling, the floors creak, and the stairs are crooked, I love this place. My grandparents spent their honeymoon here. As a child my father spent his vacations here with his family. Until I was eleven, this was the only vacation spot I knew. How much longer Crandall's Lodge will stand and be used, I don't know. But I do know that in my heart there will always be a spot for Crandall's Lodge, traditional vacation place of my family.

SHARON BALDWIN
13 years of age
Elkhart, Indiana
September 23, 1966

(Thought this might interest you.)

By the early 1940s, when this aerial view was taken— possibly during a drought year to demonstrate that the deep beaches had returned—Crandall's Lodge stands mostly alone, with the barn in the background. Crandall's Barn was the scene of private events and numerous adult and teenage dances. Reportedly, it was a stop for bootleggers taking advantage of Minnesota's more liberal liquor laws in the days after Prohibition.

This testimonial letter speaks to the love that guests had for the musty Crandall's Lodge. Dale and Bob Flemming ran Crandall's Lodge starting in 1946, operating it for nearly three decades. In 1974, it was purchased by Vernal Keerbs, who dismantled it early in 1976, bringing an end to the resort after 104 years of operation. Private homes stand on the property today.

About a year after Orlando Crandall built his hotel, W.D. Sampson built a hotel on property one mile east, about where Mini-Wakan State Park is today. Sampson's lodge was often complimented for the natural beauty that surrounded it. Sampson's Lodge fiercely competed with Crandall's by offering free fishing tackle and boats. Every year, Sampson made the annual opening of his modest hotel into an event, hosting picnics with entertainment and free steamboat rides well into the night. Sampson moved to Des Moines after only a couple of years but secured well-known local farmer George P. Wodell and his wife, Loues, to operate the resort. Sampson's Lodge closed around 1911, and the lumber was reportedly repurposed to create a smaller vacation cabin nearby.

Iowa was the frontier in the 1870s, and that attracted all sorts of entrepreneurs, including Englishman Billy Lillywhite, who, in 1872, built a lodge on the "old Indian trail" along the west side of Spirit Lake. Lillywhite Lodge was a regular stop on the stagecoach line between Spirit Lake and Jackson, Minnesota—which was the closest rail terminal until 1882, when rail service began at the south end of Big Spirit Lake. Lillywhite sold the lodge in 1875 (and again in 1881, so the earlier deal must not have been completed).

WEST SIDE HOTEL TO BE TORN DOWN—LUMBER SOLD

The West Side Hotel, on the south shore of big Spirit lake, now owned by a Mason City corporation, is now being taken down and the lumber sold. Phil Timpe has charge of the work and disposal of the lumber.

The West Side hotel was in its origin was built about 65 years ago. The original section was what was known as the Lilly White hotel and stood about where the Denecke cottage now stands and was owned by an English taxidermist, Billy Lilly White. It was later moved to the present location and added to and during its day has been one of the popular stopping places for hunters and fishermen in the lakes region.

Known well into the 1920s as a quiet fisherman's retreat, the West Side Hotel was owned over the years by Vilas Arnold, Joe Wanninger, and others. It stood until 1934, by which time it must have been viewed as an outdated anachronism. No doubt it had small, sparsely furnished rooms and, like other pioneer-era buildings, was likely drafty. Unlike other early resorts, it included little—if any—excess land that could be sold for cash flow.

Two

HOTEL ORLEANS

"Magnificence was the keynote," reporters gushed when the Hotel Orleans opened in 1883. The Burlington, Cedar Rapids & Northern Railway had pushed service through to Spirit Lake in June the previous year, and part and parcel with the railroad's plan was the construction of a grand hotel on the south shore of Spirit Lake—the Hotel Orleans.

And grand it was, offering spectacular views from its four-story-high rooftop deck with seven pennant-waving spires, a bowling alley, the finest dining, private baths, and spacious guest rooms that opened to wide verandas for catching lake breezes. The grandeur was not to last. The Hotel Orleans was built when Big Spirit Lake was at a high point, and over the next 14 years, lake levels dropped nearly eight feet; everyone feared the lake was drying up. Other factors contributed to its closing, including increasing prohibitions against liquor consumption and what was known as the Panic of 1893, which devastated the upper class in general and railroads in particular. Following a ruinous windstorm, the magnificent structure was closed in 1898 and torn down in 1899.

Beginning in 1906, four more Orleans hotels were erected on the same property, each one smaller and less pretentious than the previous one. The final Hotel Orleans, owned by the widow of the hotelier who built the last version in 1936, was converted into a private residence. A large, modern home now stands on the site next to the Orleans beach and the Spirit Lake spillway.

> The B., C. R. & N. Railroad Company is quietly going forward to conquer new territory, having definitely determined to extend its line from Clarion to Spirit Lake. This Spirit Lake country is said to be among the most beautiful and attractive in the northwest; so much so that when it can be reached by rail it must make a ppoular summer resort.

In 1881, the *Cedar Rapids Times* newspaper reported that the Burlington, Cedar Rapids & Northern Railway (BCR&N) not only had designs on completing rail service to northwest Iowa, it also foreshadowed the business the railroad hoped to generate by transporting vacationing passengers to the region. A year later, in June 1882, the city of Spirit Lake was jubilant at the opening of new service.

The BCR&N revealed plans for a grand hotel at the south end of Big Spirit Lake. The Hotel Orleans would have stunning rooms, turrets with spires, pathways to promenade, docks and bathhouses (changing houses), and its own steamship—the *Queen*. The engraving on this letterhead represents a refined version of the *Queen*; early promotional drawings showed a Mississippi River–type paddleboat, probably because engravers utilized an image from other resorts.

HOTEL ORLEANS

After several hours of riding the train through prairie and small towns, weary passengers must have had their breath taken away by the vision that greeted them at Spirit Lake. The Hotel Orleans' four stories with spires and pennants blowing in the breeze, well-manicured grounds, and an immense dining hall made it an attractive and memorable destination. It was also conveniently located only steps from the rail platform. One can presume, based on hand-colored prints made in later years, that the Hotel Orleans was white- or cream-colored with green trim and redbrick roof shingles. The uppermost deck was used for viewing the lake and surrounding area. The hotel's most notable feature was the 16-foot-wide veranda on the upper levels. Guests could enjoy fresh air during afternoon strolls, and every room opened to the breezes, which enabled flow-through ventilation in the days before air conditioning.

HOTEL ORLEANS.

Formal Opening of the Largest Hotel in Iowa.

The Occasion Lent Additional Attraction by the Presence of Distinguished Guests From Georgia.

Full Description of the House, the Excursion and the Opening Exercises.

On June 22, 1883, opening ceremonies for the Hotel Orleans were first-rate and spared no expense. Delegations of banking and rail officials from Cedar Rapids were accompanied by speakers from as far away as Georgia—including that state's governor, James S. Boynton. One of the guest speakers was Capt. C.B. Richards of Fort Dodge, who was part of the relief party that arrived following the 1857 Spirit Lake Massacre. Instead of a 10-day march across trackless prairie, he remarked, that same trip by rail required only four hours "in a palace car."

This photograph from 1884, taken from the southern end of the isthmus between Spirit Lake and East Okoboji, shows the true size of the hotel. At 324 feet long by 40 feet wide, the main building easily dwarfed any other hotel in the state. A 60-by-120-foot addition (on the right) extended nearly to the railroad track. The dining room alone measured 50 by 60 feet.

The Hotel Orleans catered to the wealthy of the upper Midwest, and reports suggest the service was first-rate and deferential. Hotel Orleans manager J.F. Hutchinson—he also managed the tony Lake Park Hotel on Lake Minnetonka in Minnesota—employed nearly 100 people at the Spirit Lake establishment by 1887. The large dining room was capable of seating upwards of 200 guests.

⇒HOTEL ⁑ ORLEANS,⇐

Spirit Lake, Iowa.

J. W. HUTCHINSON, Proprietor.

This photograph likely dates from the Hotel Orleans opening week in 1883, when promoters had special pennants flying in the breeze. Taken from the high turret and looking west, the picture shows guests enjoying spectacular rooftop views from the edge of Big Spirit Lake. Railroad service was just one year in, and at this time, there was virtually no building on the lake's south end.

Local photographer L.F. Williamz captured the dominating appearance of the Hotel Orleans on Big Spirit Lake. Taken on a quiet day from a boat in about 1895, the image includes many of the elements shown on the engraving on page 20. At left, pulled ashore for the winter, is a bathhouse with enclosed areas for changing. In the center is the steamer *Queen*, along with a covered storehouse. To the right is the railroad's water tower, and the low structure next to the

tower may be the resort's own gas-manufacturing plant, which was utilized to provide lighting. At the far right is a boathouse for rowboat, bait, and tackle sales. Note the amount of visible sand beach. Big Spirit's water levels dropped every year—as much as eight feet—after the hotel was constructed. Hotel management feared the lake would dry up. (Courtesy of the Dickinson County Historical Museum.)

The Hotel Orleans had its own boats not only for guest use but also to catch fresh fish. In this picture taken next to a sturdy Spirit Lake dock sometime after 1900, a man fishing from this gasoline-powered launch is shown with an eight-pound lunker worthy of being photographed. Both largemouth and smallmouth bass are species of black bass.

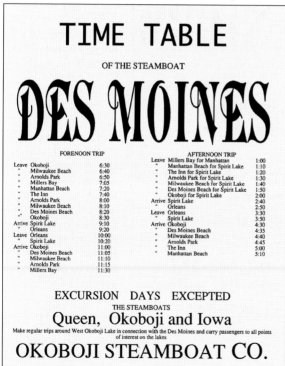

TIME TABLE

OF THE STEAMBOAT

DES MOINES

FORENOON TRIP			AFTERNOON TRIP		
			Leave Millers Bay for Manhattan		1:00
Leave	Okoboji	6:30	" Manhattan Beach for Spirit Lake		1:10
"	Milwaukee Beach	6:40	" The Inn for Spirit Lake		1:20
"	Arnolds Park	6:50	" Arnolds Park for Spirit Lake		1:30
"	Millers Bay	7:05	" Milwaukee Beach for Spirit Lake		1:40
"	Manhattan Beach	7:20	" Des Moines Beach for Spirit Lake		1:50
"	The Inn	7:40	" Okoboji for Spirit Lake		2:00
"	Arnolds Park	8:00	Arrive Spirit Lake		2:40
"	Milwaukee Beach	8:10	" Orleans		2:50
"	Des Moines Beach	8:20	Leave Orleans		3:30
"	Okoboji	8:30	" Spirit Lake		3:50
Arrive	Spirit Lake	9:10	Arrive Okoboji		4:30
"	Orleans	9:20	" Des Moines Beach		4:35
Leave	Orleans	10:00	" Milwaukee Beach		4:40
"	Spirit Lake	10:20	" Arnolds Park		4:45
Arrive	Okoboji	11:00	" The Inn		5:00
"	Des Moines Beach	11:05	" Manhattan Beach		5:10
"	Milwaukee Beach	11:10			
"	Arnolds Park	11:15			
"	Millers Bay	11:30			

EXCURSION DAYS EXCEPTED

THE STEAMBOATS

Queen, Okoboji and Iowa

Make regular trips around West Okoboji Lake in connection with the Des Moines and carry passengers to all points of interest on the lakes

OKOBOJI STEAMBOAT CO.

Hotel Orleans may have had its own steamboat, but other steamboat operators also began shuttling visitors to and from the other Okoboji lakes. This c. 1910 schedule shows that the steamer *Des Moines* was busy during the summer months, traveling all around West Okoboji en route to the hotel. Early steamer operators Satchwell Elmer Mills and Calvin "Cars" Mills, along with Fred Roff, eventually came to own the Okoboji fleet.

Numerous factors contributed to the demise of the Hotel Orleans: the financial Panic of 1893 devastated the wealthy and the railroad stocks they owned; years of cool summers; and fears that Spirit Lake would dry up were chief among them. Additionally, growing interest in the prohibition of alcohol and reports of violations, as shown at right in 1899, tarnished the hotel's image.

The work of tearing down the Hotel Orleans at Spirit Lake is now going on. The west wing as far as the office will be removed this spring and the entire structure will be torn down this fall. The building cost the company $120,000 and its removal is regretted The magnificent hotel attracted visitors from all parts of the country during the time it was operated, vhich was only during the summer season. A few years ago the proprietors w.re arrested because liquor was being sold ont he premises, and it is said that these persecutions led the owners io determine upon removing the hotel The managers offered to resume business this season if they would be granted protection, but this was not forthcoming, and the removal of the building is the result. It is a great loss to the Spirit Lake summer resort, and by some is regarded as a calamity.

VOLUME 16--NO. 189.

A FEARFUL STORM

Two Lives Lost and a Million Dollar Damage Done to Buildings and Grain by the Hurricane Which Swept Territory a Hundred Miles Long by Forty

Wide in Northwestern Iowa, the Spirit Lake Country and Southern Minnesota Last Friday Evening---First Authentic Account---Details of the

Damage Done to Cottages and Other Buildings Around Spirit Lake, Okoboji and Adjoining Country---Many Narrow Escapes---Wallace's Battle With Capsized Sailboat.

The Worst Ever Known There.

If there was a coup de grâce, it was an 1898 windstorm that severely damaged the hotel. The headlines at left (from the *Cedar Rapids Gazette*) hint at the severity—much of the verandas and roof were removed. It is arguable, however, that the original mortgagee for the Orleans, banker and railroad director Lyman Cook, kept the hotel open through lean years. He was a frequent visitor, and the hotel may have been his pet project. When he died in 1898, it was announced shortly thereafter that the hotel would not reopen.

New Orleans Hotel, Spirit Lake, Iowa.

Around six years after the Hotel Orleans closed, a "New" Orleans Hotel was erected on the same spot at the foot of Big Spirit Lake. John Burmeister, a hotel operator who had bought the Crandall House in Spirit Lake a few years earlier, erected this hotel in 1906. It was much smaller than the original Orleans at 182 feet by 38 feet with an L-shaped addition. Offering 72 rooms, the New Orleans Hotel featured a ballroom, restaurant, and 10-foot verandas for fresh air. It was located just steps from the rail platform that, in 1903, became part of the Chicago, Rock Island & Pacific line. This building was not long-lived and burned to the ground in January 1908 along with a small saloon to the east of it. Burmeister promised to rebuild and started construction almost immediately on a new hotel.

New Orleans Hotel, Spirit Lake, Iowa.

Unlike the first Hotel Orleans, the New Orleans Hotel was clearly less ostentatious and was focused on providing a relaxing waterfront vacation. The horse-and-buggy era was quickly giving way to motorcars, and railroad service—although convenient for an Iowa Great Lakes vacation—was beginning to diminish in importance. This postcard of the 1906 hotel shows not just guests and boats but likely many locals arriving in their carriages.

1403   The New Orleans Hotel, Spirit Lake, Ia.   HANSON-ULLBERG CO., MINNEAPOLIS

This rare postcard view of the 1906 hotel shows it just steps from the lake, which, by this time, had filled to its normal level. Water is visible on the right, along with a pile of lumber—most likely dock materials. Wide verandas were still an important attraction for guests, and what may be a saloon is visible in the foreground.

After the New Orleans Hotel burned down in 1908, owner/operator John Burmeister either sold his interests to a friend, Guy Burnside of Knoxville, Illinois, or partnered with him, since Burnside had also taken over the Antlers Hotel in town. Burnside ran this version of the hotel, which had 56 sleeping rooms, until his death in 1930. Guy Burnside's widow, Mabel, operated it for several years after he died.

The 1909 Orleans Hotel (the name preferred by Guy Burnside) favored a broad expanse of lawn leading to the sandy beach. At right in this photograph is a portion of the dance pavilion, which was built close to the shoreline to catch cool lake breezes. This view looks west, with the small, dark building in the middle offering a shady retreat apart from dances.

With access available by rail, automobile, steamboat, and private launch, the Orleans Hotel established itself as a convenient focal point of activity on Spirit Lake. In addition to the large and popular lakeside dancing pavilion, guests could spend time in this screened cabana to relax. At lower right, a portion of a tennis net is visible.

Fire struck the Orleans for the fourth time on July 3, 1936. After it began near a chimney by the kitchen, the blaze destroyed the top floor and most of the second floor of the hotel. Not one of the 30 registered guests was harmed, and hotel operator Mabel Burnside and her clerk helped remove personal belongings along with the hotel's records and cash boxes.

Operator Mabel Burnside initially reported the hotel would not be rebuilt after the 1936 fire and said a small-cabin colony would be constructed. Burnside changed her mind and had the 1910 hotel remodeled into this considerably smaller building. The Orleans Hotel continued operating, along with the adjacent Sail Inn tearoom, for some years after the fire.

The Orleans shown above was operated by the F.E. Weatherly family beginning in 1939. The Nick Girg family bought the hotel in 1948 and ran the establishment until it passed into private hands in 1955, as this real estate advertisement suggests. The building then became a private residence. It is now gone and has been replaced by a larger modern home.

Three

TEMPLAR PARK

In the latter decades of the 19th century, fraternal organizations were commensurate with status, and cities vied to host their annual meetings. Thus, in 1885, when the Grand Commandry of Iowa, Knights Templar, chose 21 acres of the Kingman farm on the west side of Big Spirit Lake for annual encampments, it was a feather in the cap for the region. Beginning in 1890, the Knights Templar and their families would hold annual conclaves on the Spirit Lake grounds. Offices, a dining room, and an "asylum" (meeting room) were built in 1891 but destroyed by a tornado in 1898. The replacement building became a full summer home for the organization with a 48-room apartment building, which was added onto with another 48 rooms and support buildings. A fire in 1917 leveled the wooden structures, but by 1919, a new fireproof building had been completed. It had 143 guest rooms, a dining room with a capacity of 200, a large rotunda, and small meeting and writing rooms for guests. A cement staircase to the lake, lakeside pavilion, and iconic gateway arch welcomed guests. Lagoons were dug and then, over time, filled in for the creation of parade grounds, a golf course, and other amenities. As interest in the fraternal society declined over the next five decades, the Knights Templar opened Templar Park to the general public, eventually running it as a "motor hotel resort" in the 1950s. The property closed in 1972 and was disposed of by the Knights Templar in 1977. The Templar Park Recreation Area was developed by the state in 1987. The lakeside stairs and grand entry arch are all that remain from the Knights Templar era.

At Templar's Park, Spirit Lake.

The fraternal organization Knights Templar, being family-friendly, had held retreats at the Iowa Great Lakes but wanted, for years, to have a permanent home here. The Knights Templar secured land on the south end of the Kingman farm on the west side of Spirit Lake in 1885, and the first conclave (gathering) was held in 1890. Bathing in Spirit Lake on a hot summer day, as shown above, quickly became a favorite activity for the Knights Templar and their families. During periods of low water during the 1890s, Templar Park's pebbly beach invited men, women, and children to take a dip. This portion of Big Spirit Lake is relatively shallow, and even children could wade out for many yards.

With the deed for 21 acres of the Kingman farm in hand, the Knights Templar wasted no time establishing it as their own. They cleared land, leveled grounds, and made the space ready for future expansion and activities. The first asylum (formal meeting room) at Templar Park was simply a tent, but offices, a dining room, and a conventional meeting room had been constructed by 1891. The members and their families camped in tents on the grounds. After a tornado destroyed the early structures in 1898, this grander and much larger building was erected the following year.

The 1899 facility was nothing if not a showplace for its time. It had two 48-room wings, a rotunda, a storeroom, a larger asylum, and a dining hall. The porch of the west wing is shown in this picture taken in 1905. In the automobile is Dr. T.B. Lacey of Council Bluffs, and the driver is Will Kistle of LeMars. Others in the photograph include Tom Adamson of LeMars and C.C. Wales of Sioux City, who is leaning against the corner of the porch. The other people in the image are unidentified.

A generation of Knights Templar used this facility until June 14, 1917, when the entire wooden structure "burned to ashes," as newspapers reported. It was thought that the building caught fire through a hole in a chimney as wastepaper was being disposed of. Most of the dining room furniture and dishes were saved. The entire building was gone in 30 or 40 minutes, according to news reports. (Courtesy of the Higgins Museum.)

After the 1917 fire, the Knights Templar quickly rebuilt, and they were not about to make the same mistake (of wooden construction). This aerial photograph shows the all-concrete fireproof building completed in 1919, which measured 365 feet long and could accommodate 384 guests. It featured a rotunda in the central area for gatherings, a large dining room for all guests, had hot and cold running water, and even had a huge 23-by-90-foot children's playroom.

This construction photograph by L.F. Williamz shows the only evidence that still remains of the magnificent Templar Park building: its stairway to the lake. Also made of concrete, these stairs were a focal point for meeting at the lakefront. After the Knights Templar sold the land in 1977, it eventually became the Templar Park State Recreation Area. In 1987, the Iowa Department of Natural Resources elected to restore the stairs for lake access.

The above scene from the late 1920s gives an idea of the commanding early-morning view guests enjoyed when staying at Templar Park. While annual weeklong conclaves were largely organized for Knights, families were free to occupy their days as vacationers for the rest of the summer. With nearly 9,000 members in the state, annual Knights Templar conclaves included parading, music, and often involved more than 500 Knights. The central portion of the building (shown below) featured a large open area for group meetings, dancing, and other events. The fireproof tile roof is clearly evident as well as the then-contemporary Spanish-influenced architecture. At the time, it was deemed pleasing to the eye and received public accolades when it was completed.

Given the time when Templar Park was built, the sunporch (above) was likely viewed as a comfortable and convivial place in which to spend time reading, playing cards, and socializing. By this time, barriers between men and women were falling, especially when people were united by the common experiences at Templar Park. The dining hall (below) appears to be clean and well-organized. It was said to fit 384 guests at once. Although it was still restricted to those in the Masonic order and their families, by the 1930s, Templar Park largely functioned as a seasonal hotel. The dining room was open to the public, however, and was well regarded for its Sunday dinners.

TEMPLAR PARK MOTOR RESORT FORMERLY TEMPLAR PARK LODGE

NOW OPEN TO THE PUBLIC — LOCATED ON WEST SHORE OF SPIRIT LAKE

6 HOLE GOLF COURSE — TENNIS

TEMPLAR DINING ROOM ALSO OPEN TO THE PUBLIC
FAMILY STYLE DINNERS — Phone 336-2588

By the 1960s, membership in the Knights Templar was dwindling, and the facility changed from the Templar Park Lodge into a motor hotel open to anyone who wished to vacation there. This advertisement from a 1967 *On the Go* tourism magazine points out the amenities, including tennis and a six-hole golf course, which was built when one of the lagoons was filled in.

TEMPLAR PARK LODGE

Templar Park Lodge certainly looked attractive in the 1970s, as this Vinton C. Arnold–produced postcard shows. However, the resort was viewed as outdated, with tiny, sparsely furnished rooms and inconvenient shared bathrooms. Added amenities like basketball and a larger golf course did not save it. Today, all that remains is the lakefront stairway and the ornate Spanish archway that served as the front gate.

Four

THE INN

James A. Beck of Fairfield was a successful hotel operator who had vacationed at Okoboji for years. According to one account, when he first conceived of the idea of a lakefront hotel on Dixon's Beach, he promised his wife he would build a small hotel of only 12 rooms—but in 1897, he built one with 24. The Inn proved to be such a success that Beck more than doubled its size in 1898, adding a long addition over the knoll to the south. Beck's hotel quickly became the social focus for Okoboji, offering the finest dining, dancing, and activities for visitors. Lakefront pavilions were built, and steamship docks were enlarged. In 1903, Beck passed management of the hotel to sisters Mary W. Jaquith and Sarah Callender, who, for four decades, became known among visitors as Aunt Polly and Aunt Sarah. Well into retirement age, the sisters sold the Inn in 1945, and a brief succession of owners eventually found the Inn too old, uncomfortable, and expensive to maintain. The original buildings were demolished in 1955–1956, and the New Inn was erected in its place. The New Inn was modern in every sense, offering contemporary motel-like rooms, air-conditioning, a swimming pool, and casual dining; guests found little to object to, and this venture succeeded for many years. Changes in ownership and management eventually saw the once-popular resort saddled with ever-increasing debt, and in 2017, banks foreclosed on the property. The 82-acre complex was sold at auction for $5.7 million, and it was razed by 2018. Five private lakefront lots were platted. The Inn's golf course has been allowed to revert to a natural prairie. As of March 2020, plans were in progress for the space to become a 70-acre public park.

Few photographs exist of the man who brought the Inn to Okoboji. James A. Beck, born in Fairfield, Iowa, in 1849, had a career that was nothing if not varied. Starting with his young man's job as a grocery clerk in 1870, he soon began his own grocery and, at age 34, leased the Leggett House hotel in Fairfield. A few years later, he leased the larger Summit House in Creston, Iowa. During that time, he also managed the John Jacob Astor House hotel on Mackinac Island, Michigan. As a man of means, he vacationed in Iowa for several years before buying land on Dixon's Beach in 1896. Beck divided his time between business interests at his home in Fairfield and Okoboji during summer months. After selling the Inn around 1910 to sisters Mary W. Jaquith and Sarah Callender, he built a sturdy, Spanish-style house on High Point on Okoboji's west side. That property was rarely occupied after James's death in 1930 (his wife, Esther, evidently did not care for it), and it eventually became a restaurant: the High Point Hacienda.

The Inn was a success from its first days in 1897. News reports from that year speak to the modest size of the first hotel building—only 24 rooms, making it little more than a lakefront rooming house—and the need for it to offer more rooms. The Inn was enlarged multiple times over the next few years. Although it is a poor reproduction, this historic photograph shows the impressive structure that greeted guests in 1897. It was a single building situated on a bluff to catch lake breezes. These holidaymakers show that vacationing at Okoboji in those days was considerably more formal than today, although boating and spending time on the sand beach remain popular activities. Note the low water level at the time—something rarely seen today.

Beck doubled the size of the Inn during its second year of operation, and it hit its stride as a major resort. For the addition, Beck managed to secure some of the interior appointments from the Hotel Orleans, which closed in 1898, just as the larger Inn was gaining popularity. The Inn succeeded while Manhattan Resort, located across the lake, faltered. Visitors to the Inn could simply step off the train at Okoboji and catch a hack to the resort; their luggage, like all that is shown here, could follow behind a short time later. Manhattan guests had to load their trunks onto a steamboat or wait for it to arrive on a wagon, which had to go around the lake.

By the time photographer L.F. Williamz took this panoramic image in 1908, the Inn was in its early heyday. The overwater pavilion at left provided guests, as well as anyone arriving by steamboat, with an airy dance hall (with dances every Monday and Thursday, as noted on the banner by the dock). The Inn Bazar, operated by J.F. Saidy, imported jewelry, clothing, Persian rugs, and *objets d'art* to catch the tourists' imaginations—and dollars. The smaller building was a shop that functioned like a modern convenience store, offering everything from clothing to film to soft drinks and snacks. It also was the concession stand for rowboat rentals and sold gasoline for the few motor launches on the lake. The Inn's broad north staircase was not only an inviting entrance to the double-arch canopy for those arriving by steamboat, but the bur oak tree growing out of it provided a novel reason to snap a quick picture.

This aerial photograph, probably from the late 1940s, illustrates the large expanse of property spanned by the Inn, with a notable feature: the curved-arch passageway. James A. Beck built the first portion (on the left of the arch) on a high knoll. The following year, he built on the knoll to the right. With the road in front, all traffic continuing north had to pass beneath this arch.

When one is a photographer who has acquired a new 1911 Brush automobile, they will find ways to show it off, and that is what L.F. Williamz did, placing his six-year-old son Evard behind the steering wheel. L.F.'s wife, Bertha, is holding Evard's baby sister, Thora. The car is emerging from beneath the Inn's pass-through arch. Lakefront driving access continued on Dixon's Beach until the early 1930s. (Courtesy of the Dickinson County Historical Museum.)

From its first days, the Inn's steamship dock provided a path for passengers to the resort's front door. The *Queen* moved from Spirit Lake in 1901, but other, smaller steamers provided service around the lakes. This view from about 1900 shows some rowboat passengers on the right, while a powered motor launch is tied up on the left side. Both J.F. Saidy's Inn Bazar and the grand staircase had yet to be built.

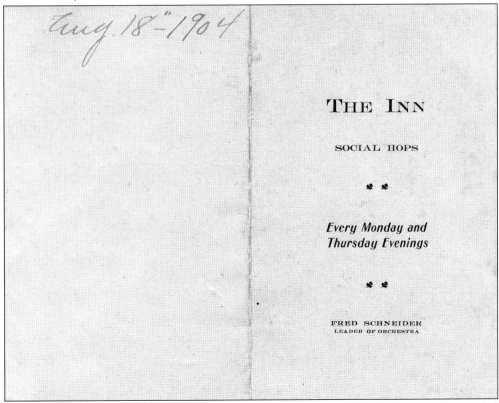

Aug. 18ᵗʰ 1904

THE INN

SOCIAL HOPS

❧ ❧

*Every Monday and
Thursday Evenings*

❧ ❧

FRED SCHNEIDER
LEADER OF ORCHESTRA

Dancing was an important and organized social convention, especially in 1904. The unidentified owner of this card filled it with the names of young men she danced with—Leslie captured most of her attention, partnering with her during waltzes, a polka, and two-step. Evidently, the Inn's house band at the time was skilled at performing a variety of popular dance tunes.

The Inn Pavilion, West Okoboji Lake, Iowa

The Inn's dancing pavilion was designed to let southerly lake breezes flow through to cool energetic dancers. Fashionable couples intent on an evening of dance could arrive by launch, steamboat, or car, making it a popular stop on the Okoboji dance hall circuit; West Lake Okoboji also had the Central Ballroom, Roof Garden, Casino, and Manhattan Ballrooms. Erected in 1900, the Inn's pavilion was removed in 1936 when overwater structures were banned.

THE
INN DANCES

THE
Tom Wells
Orchestra
OF MASON CITY, Will Furnish Music

Dances Every Monday, Thursday, Saturday Nights

THROUGHOUT THE ENTIRE SEASON

Free Matinee Dance on Wednesday Afternoon From 3:30 to 5:00 P. M.

Children Especially Welcomed

Orchestras like the one mentioned in this advertisement provided music for dancers in 1923. The Tom Wells Orchestra was well-known in the 1920s, sometimes playing for several weeks at a time in dance halls in Okoboji, Clear Lake, Emmetsburg, and Estherville, as well as making one-night appearances throughout the state. A music teacher, Wells played clarinet and saxophone, and the group also had three horns, a piano, drums, a xylophone, and a violin.

In addition to being a fashionable place to vacation, dine, and dance, the Inn provided boats for rental or pleasure sailing. Art Bowles of Storm Lake posed for this c. 1936 photograph in front of the Inn Bazar gift shop. With his high boots, he appears to be dressed for some shoreline fishing and was likely about to try his luck in deeper water from the boat—which, during the Depression, would have been an expenditure. An avid fisherman, Bowles, in his later years, spent two weeks every summer vacationing with friends and family members at the Iowa Great Lakes, chiefly at the Manhattan Cottages or Vacation Village.

The Inn, pictured above in 1913, showed no signs at that time of the changes that would soon occur. The overwater pavilion, Inn Bazar, and gift shop were removed by 1936, the main road no longer passed in front of the resort, and the *Queen* became purely an excursion boat in the 1920s (but the Inn remained a regular stop). Below, the advertisement in a 1941 *Atlas of the Iowa Great Lakes* presented all the Inn had to offer: 100 rooms, cottages, dining, boating, swimming, and diving. The Inn had peaked in terms of popularity by the 1940s and was beginning to be seen as antiquated. Importantly, owners Sarah Callender and Mary Jaquith—Aunt Sarah and Aunt Polly, to regular visitors—were nearing retirement age in the 1940s. They sold the Inn in 1945, and the Inn's post–World War II owners were poised to make changes for a new, more youthful customer base.

BEACH CLUB - THE INN - OKOBOJI SPRINGS IOWA.

A.R. Johnson, who bought the Inn in 1945, spent considerable effort to rejuvenate the resort for future guests. In addition to remodeling the lobby and improving room amenities, he oversaw the opening of the Beach Club café, which featured a new casual-dining menu. Specialties were fish or chicken, which could be packed for picnics.

In the days when dining out was a relatively infrequent occurrence, meals at the Beach Club were varied to attract guests. The fare ranged from fried chicken and liver with onions to foie gras and lobster tails. This menu from 1954 speaks to the traditional American diet, but "fast food" was about to enter the scene.

Beach Club Dinner Suggestions

Something old, something new, a little different than others have served you.

Soupe Bon Homme or Grapefruit Juice
Summer Salad
French Fried or Hashed O'Brien Potatoes
Vegetable   Mixed Breads & Butter
Dessert   Beverage

Roast Leg o Fresh Pork, apple compute 1.00
Grilled Baby Beef Liver, smothered with onions ... 95c
Broiled Banger Bay Lobster Tails, drawn butter _ 1.50
Roast Sirloin of Baby Beef, brown gravy 90c
Fried Filet of Ocean Catfish, Maitre D'Hotel 1.00

1.15   Our Chef's Featured Dishes   1.15
Chicken in a Basket
Local raised spring chicken southern fried to a tempting golden brown, heaps of french fries.
Hot Bread   Coffee
Eaten the natural way—silverware served upon request only

1.25   The Beachcomber   1.25
Pate de Fois Gras (choice chicken livers in the delectable style made famous by the world's foremost master chefs)
Choice of Dinner Line.

85c   The Gourmet's Life Raft   85c
(An ordinary dish made extraordinarily delicious)
Fried Golden Cornmeal Mush and Homemade Sausage
Choice of Dinner Line

1.20   Treasures of the Deep   1.20
A colorful plate containing a healthful selection of four of the deep sea's choicest morsels—choice of dinner line.

Pies, cakes and French pastries baked in our own ovens.

Bridge Teas Every Tuesday and Friday from 2 to 4:30 P. M.
Refreshments

An unidentified man makes a telephone call from a public telephone booth in this photograph probably taken around 1954. Although this scene may have seemed unremarkable at the time, everything in this photo is now gone. The Inn in the background and its successor, the New Inn, have been razed; telephone booths are now a quaint curiosity; and the parking area next to the booth became a cul-de-sac.

Old-timers decried the changes, but the original Inn building was demolished in 1955–1956 and replaced by the New Inn in 1957. This postcard of the main lobby entrance in the New Inn's early years speaks to the cultural changes—the 1950s and 1960s saw guests embracing modern amenities, and the New Inn was designed to appeal to them.

Guests stroll next to the New Inn's heated outdoor swimming pool. The New Inn offered motel-style buildings with modern conveniences like private baths and air-conditioning. Many of the 100 rooms were enlarged in subsequent years, more rooms were added, and before long, a convention center was built to accompany the nine-hole, par-three golf links, driving range, and miniature golf course. All were lighted for nighttime play.

By 1967, the New Inn had grown to 130 rooms and even provided entertainment for families and conventioneers. With other resorts around the lakes now catering to families, the New Inn fell in line, offering childcare and supervised activities for children. The adjacent Spirit Lake airport enabled some businessmen to fly in, play a round of golf or go fishing, have a meeting, and fly home all in one day.

This photograph shows William Hahn of Omaha and his five-year-old daughter Denise staying at the New Inn in 1965. The rooms at the New Inn look familiar today, but to some visitors—especially children—they were the height of modern comfort. Aluminum windows and through-wall air conditioners kept vacationers comfortable when lake breezes failed.

Even with other activities available for children, such as miniature golf, West Okoboji still attracted children to the New Inn's docks. Five-year-old Denise Hawn is shown getting comfortable on one of the resort's diving boards while her father looks on. At one time, beginning in 1924, the Inn held annual swimming and diving competitions in which locals and vacationers could compete with staff from resorts around the lakes.

From its first days, the New Inn featured top-quality entertainment. This 1967 local *Visitor* magazine advertisement speaks to the variety of vocal and instrumental groups that performed at the resort. Notable is Marilyn Maye, who continued to perform annually at the Okoboji venue and beyond. After the Inn was razed in 2018, she performed at the local Pearson Lakes Art Center—at age 90—to a sold-out house.

Pictured in 1971 at the New Inn dock are 11-year-old Carol Gorman (left) and her sister Jane Gorman, age 13. The John E. Gorman family from Winterset, Iowa, vacationed every year at the New Inn. The sisters' grandparents, Marion and John C. Gorman, originally met at the Great Lakes area and also stayed at the Inn every summer. Multigenerational family gatherings continue to be an Okoboji tradition.

The Inn property is pictured here in 2017 at the end of its last season. The Inn, which had grown to 155 units among several buildings, closed for good in December 2017 after being sold at a foreclosure auction. It sold for $5.7 million to Whitecap LLC, an investor group with Okoboji ties. In addition to the valuable lakefront footage, the deal included about 69 acres of golf course

and farmland across the road. The new owners set up an arrangement for the golf course and farmland to be preserved from development in perpetuity to help preserve neighborhood green space. As of this writing, all of the lakefront lots have been sold.

This picture—taken from the second story of the Inn during demolition—shows the great view of West Okoboji afforded by the resort. In front of the swimming pool were single-level, motel-style buildings, while two-story units once stood on the open ground to the right on both sides of the street. At the time of its closing in December 2017, the Inn had 155 rooms.

The demolition of the Inn revealed some unusual artifacts, such as this brick wall. Beginning around 1990, this wall located near the kitchen—far away from guests' eyes—was "signed" by employees. Traditionally, they would do this on their last day of summer employment. This image shows just a part of that wall, which included the signatures of chefs, kitchen help, servers, security personnel, and housekeeping and office employees. The last signature was added in 2017.

Tearing down a landmark like the Inn was neither easy nor swift. The sale was completed in December 2017, and demolition began almost immediately. This April 2018 image shows the main building just days before it was finally razed. This structure had many renovations since 1957, and in addition to poolside spaces, it contained the lobby, main hotel offices, gift shop, kitchen, dining room, and a large meeting room. Eight lakefront motel-style buildings had been removed, and crews labored to do the same with four two-story units to the west. Demolition and land-leveling continued throughout 2018 as the Columns iconic structure was torn down and golf pro shop, tennis courts, and playground were removed.

The ghostlike words "THE INN" were barely visible on the main building's lake-facing facade just days before it was torn down. After 121 years of hosting vacationers, family reunions, and business conventions and providing stirring entertainment, sumptuous meals, recreational activities of every stripe, and lakefront fun on West Okoboji, the Inn passed into history in 2018.

Five

MANHATTAN

Following the arrival of rail service in 1882, it was clear things were going to be happening at Okoboji. The once-remote Spirit Lake resorts no longer appeared so distant. Wesley Arnold's rooming house in Arnolds Park would soon give way to a hotel and tourist-attracting amusements, and investors like D.B. Lyon of Des Moines saw opportunity on the west side of Okoboji. After purchasing hundreds of lakefront acres with a sandy point and nearly a mile of shoreline in 1892, Lyon hoped the Manhattan Beach resort would appeal to those looking for relaxation on West Okoboji. Lyon quickly organized a stock company and began selling lots. Its lack of access proved to be a fatal flaw—roads on the west side of Okoboji were few and of poor quality. Lyon saw the Hotel Orleans offering steamboat service to visitors and realized his Manhattan Beach resort should offer it, too. An old steamer, *Ben Lennox*, was purchased and quickly renamed *Manhattan*. In addition to bathing, the resort offered first-class dining and entertainment as well as more exciting activities, like a water toboggan slide. Each hotel room had a view of the lake, and the amenities were first-rate: a bathhouse, a dancing pavilion, a restaurant, and even a bowling alley. However, the initial venture was too remote to succeed. Cash-generating lots failed to sell, and the venture went bankrupt in 1899. Other entrepreneurs jumped in, and for two decades, Manhattan vied with the Inn for tourists and social events. As more people began buying lakeside property for vacation homes, business fell off, and the resort struggled until 1933, when it was made into a cottage colony, and the hotel was demolished.

Rumors swirled for weeks in 1892 about activity on West Okoboji's west shore. Finally, the *Cedar Rapids Evening Gazette* announced that a group of investors headed by D.B. Lyon of Des Moines had purchased a mile and a half of shoreline to develop the Manhattan Beach resort. In addition to a launching a waterside entertainment venue, the investors also planned to sell cottage lots. When it opened in July 1892, the resort offered a sand beach, a dancing pavilion, a third-floor viewing platform, a lakefront band performance stage, and 32 changing rooms for bathers (swimmers). Tennis courts and a bowling alley were soon added, as well as a café and a thrilling water toboggan slide.

The grand opening of the Manhattan on July 1, 1892, was designed to attract people not only from the community but from all over the state. Free steamship rides on the freshly christened *Manhattan* were offered in an attempt to draw crowds from the Arnolds Park railroad station. Speakers included Iowa Supreme Court judge Josiah Given, a local celebrity—he built the first "vacation cottage" in Okoboji in 1886. The unusual angle of this photograph taken in the Manhattan's early days gives a clue to what D.B. Lyon thought would appeal to vacationers. Wide verandas extended all around the pavilion on two levels to catch lake breezes. The hotel being built over the sandbar meant that guests were only steps away from West Okoboji's clear waters.

Other resorts on Spirit Lake, like the Hotel Orleans, had a steamer for guest convenience, but in Manhattan's case, it was a necessity. Okoboji's remote west side had few roads, and virtually all guests used steamboats to come and go. The *Ben Lennox*, launched at Okoboji in 1884, was purchased by investors and renamed the *Manhattan* in time for the opening. Unreliable and poorly maintained, the vessel only lasted until 1899.

TOBOGGAN SLIDE — MANHATTAN BEACH

This 1895 tourist booklet photo shows the resort's many attractions. Manhattan offered a covelike beach with shallow water suitable for wading, a deep steamboat dock (with two steamships tied up), and a thrilling water toboggan slide, which was practically required for resorts of the day. Despite all this, the Manhattan investors realized they needed to sell lots in order to make the resort profitable.

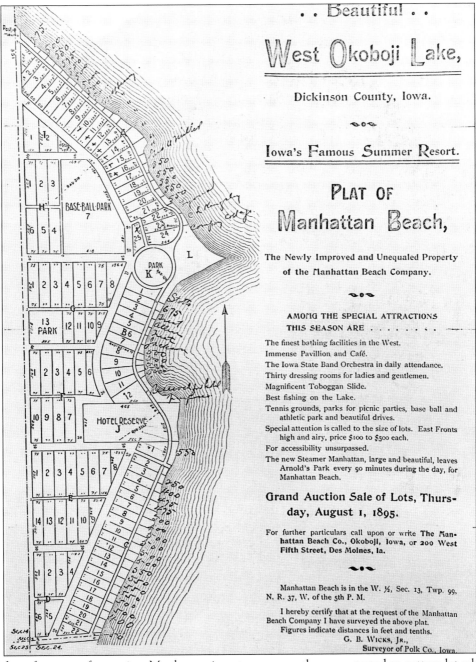

.. Beautiful ..

West Okoboji Lake,

Dickinson County, Iowa.

❧❀❧

Iowa's Famous Summer Resort.

PLAT OF

Manhattan Beach,

The Newly Improved and Unequaled Property
of the Manhattan Beach Company.

❧❀❧

AMONG THE SPECIAL ATTRACTIONS
THIS SEASON ARE . . . .

The finest bathing facilities in the West.

Immense Pavillion and Café.

The Iowa State Band Orchestra in daily attendance.

Thirty dressing rooms for ladies and gentlemen.

Magnificent Toboggan Slide.

Best fishing on the Lake.

Tennis grounds, parks for picnic parties, base ball and
athletic park and beautiful drives.

Special attention is called to the size of lots. East Fronts
high and airy, price $100 to $500 each.

For accessibility unsurpassed.

The new Steamer Manhattan, large and beautiful, leaves
Arnold's Park every 50 minutes during the day, for
Manhattan Beach.

Grand Auction Sale of Lots, Thursday, August 1, 1895.

For further particulars call upon or write The Manhattan Beach Co., Okoboji, Iowa, or 200 West Fifth Street, Des Moines, Ia.

❧❀❧

Manhattan Beach is in the W. ½, Sec. 13, Twp. 99, N. R. 37, W. of the 5th P. M.

I hereby certify that at the request of the Manhattan Beach Company I have surveyed the above plat. Figures indicate distances in feet and tenths.
G. B. WICKS, JR.,
Surveyor of Polk Co., Iowa.

After a few years of operation, Manhattan investors apparently concentrated on cottage lot sales. Beyond bringing money in from sales, having neighbors would aid in ongoing cash flow, too. Despite a presumably reasonable price of $100 to $500, the mile and a half of shoreline attracted only about a dozen buyers. Poor access no doubt depressed sales. This flyer from 1895 takes pains to romanticize the offerings (offering "the finest bathing facilities in the West" for example, along with identifying the *Manhattan* steamship as "large and beautiful"). The investors also planned to build a baseball field and other parks for picnics. A bowling alley was added to complement the tennis courts. (Courtesy of the Dickinson County Museum.)

By 1898, the resort was in deep financial trouble, and creditors forced a sheriff's sale to satisfy growing debts. A succession of new managers and owners, beginning with Joseph Myerly of Des Moines, tried their luck at bringing and retaining guests. Myerly formed the Manhattan Hotel & Land Company with his sons in 1900 to handle land sales and the development of the resort. Myerly's ownership sparked construction on the point. With renewed life, the Manhattan Resort expanded, as shown in this c. 1910 photograph. The pavilion was enclosed, and a new hotel was built over the point. One newspaper said, "It now has accommodations for 250 guests . . . and a porch 300 feet long facing the most beautiful portion of the lake and affording a promenade in all kinds of weather." A billiard hall and electric light plant were also added.

State newspapers like the *Cedar Rapids Evening Gazette* predicted that a rail line on the west side of the lake was "a certainty," and there is no doubt that it was a factor in Joseph Myerly's planned development. No rail line was built, and Myerly sold Manhattan in 1915. It continued to struggle through the 1910s and 1920s until roads improved. Local photographer L.F. Williamz knew what attracted people to Okoboji, and he captured it. This 1910 photograph taken by Williamz shows a group of vacationers on an exciting ride in the *Falcon*, one of West Okoboji's excursion sailboats, as it glided past the Manhattan Resort. Both the *Falcon* and the *Golden Rule* were gone by the late 1920s as sailing fell out of favor for tourist transportation.

Manhattan Beach Hotel

453

ON WEST OKOBOJI LAKE
R. F. D. 4, Spirit Lake, Iowa

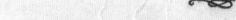

—AMERICAN PLAN $21.00 per week per person.

—EUROPEAN PLAN $10.50 per week per person.

—EUROPEAN PLAN $12.50 per week two persons.

Midway Between Two Good Golf Courses

Very Fine Beach   -:-   Home Cooking

Regular Boat Service

WE AIM TO PLEASE . . . . M. TEMPLE

A succession of new owners and managers battled dwindling attendance at the Manhattan as the 1920s drew to a close. More frequent dances and even repositioning the resort as a dining destination (Sunday dinners were a specialty) did little to salvage the business. This card from the era shows the costs for the European plan—meaning no food included—and the American plan, in which meals were built into the room rate. The beginning of the Depression spelled the end of the Manhattan Beach resort. A frequent guest, Hobart A. Ross, once chatted on the dock with a man who turned out to be the resort's receiver. Before long, a valuation was agreed upon. Ross bought the resort and, in 1933, had it dismantled, using the lumber to build 25 quaint guest cottages.

This aerial photograph shows the Manhattan Beach sand point without the old hotel, water toboggan slide, or dance hall. Instead, the broad beach has been turned into an open area, with only a few of the cottages visible among the oak trees. By this time this photograph was taken in the early 1940s, the Manhattan Beach resort had been reduced to about 20 acres in size.

Advertised as "modern" cottages—meaning they had electricity and indoor plumbing—these quaint buildings were still largely made of used lumber. On cold days, guests would shiver, as there was little, if any, insulation. That did not deter vacationers in the least, as Manhattan quickly became a family vacation destination. Hobart Ross owned the resort until 1948, when he sold it to Nic Kamp of LeMars. Kamp operated it until 1957.

Families at Manhattan usually booked for the following summer before checking out. Little Alan Bowles of Storm Lake, Iowa, is shown at left in the mid-1950s with his father's friend Russell Settlemeyer. These two families were devoted to fishing and vacationed together for years. Bowles recalls storing their cane fishing poles beneath the rental cottage at vacation's end and retrieving them, undisturbed over the winter, again the following year.

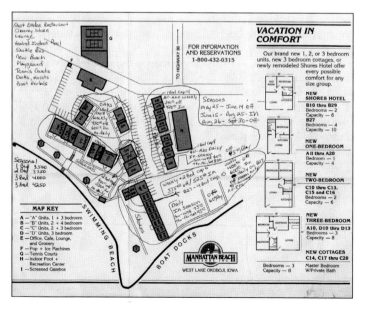

Nic Kamp sold Manhattan to a group of investors who sought to introduce then-new condominiums, which never happened. Instead, M.L. "Chick" Evans operated the resort until selling to Dick Fedora in 1975. While Fedora made many improvements, the resort layout changed substantially when Chuck Long purchased it in 1984 and replaced the old wooden cottages with attached cottages and motel-style rooms.

Six

CRESCENT BEACH

The story of Crescent Beach must be told from its earliest days, when nearly 1,000 acres between Eagle Point and Gull Point were developed into an area called Lakewood Park. James A. Beck, who had built the Inn some years before, envisioned an "American Venice" with canals, lagoons, rustic bridges, and perhaps even gondolas to delight visitors. In 1911, Beck found additional investors, platted the area for more than 500 lots, and brought in two dredges to carve out more than three miles of canals. However, with numerous lakefront lots readily available elsewhere, Lakewood Park failed to achieve anything close to Beck's dream. Only a few lots sold. Beck built the Crescent Beach Hotel in 1914 to attract visitors to this quiet portion of Emerson Bay but sold his interests to partners two years later. W.A. White then managed the property, eventually adding cottages and making it more family-friendly. At the end of World War II, the resort was sold to Carroll Lane, who added to the available cottages, rooms, and amenities for decades. In the 1970s, the Crescent Beach Resort changed hands. All but a small portion of the original 1,000 feet of beachfront land was eventually sold for cottages, and a new, modern—but considerably smaller—hotel called the Thunderbird Lodge remained.

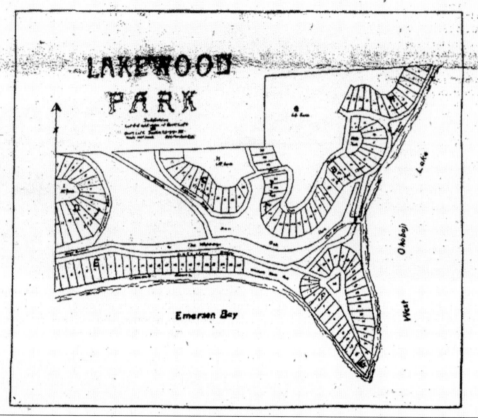

Any discussion of Crescent Beach has to begin with Lakewood Park, the original business undertaking at that location, which extended from Miller's Bay on the north to Emerson Bay on the south. James A. Beck (founder of the Inn) and Spirit Lake real estate broker H.E. Mills began buying property around Eagle Point in 1907. In 1911, Beck convinced other investors, including Inn operator Mary W. Jaquith, to put money into a venture across the lake—Lakewood Park. Beck's vision involved canals being dug and the establishment of an "American Venice" with parkland for picnics, lazy lagoons, rustic bridges, a Dutch windmill with a second-floor reading room, and perhaps even gondolas. With more than 300 acres and lakefront land around Eagle Point at his disposal, Beck hoped to quickly sell 500 platted lots for vacation homes. However, with many lakefront lots commonly available elsewhere on West Okoboji, his venture did not go as planned.

James A. Beck hired dredges to carve out nearly three miles of canals between Miller's Bay and Emerson Bay. The steam-powered Fairbanks floating dredge, shown here just east of Eagle Point, could remove up to 2,000 cubic yards of dirt per day, newspapers reported, and with electric lights, it could work all through the night. The entrances on the bays are still in use today. (Courtesy of the Higgins Museum.)

The Lakewood Park area was hardly enticing in 1912, even as James A. Beck arrived on the scene to supervise progress. Here, just north of Eagle Point, the shore was barely above water level and was strewn with many rocks and scrub trees. Beck and his investors tried to sell as many lots as they could, but it was slow going due to poor access and few amenities in the area. (Courtesy of the Higgins Museum.)

Although many Lakewood Park lots did sell, James A. Beck and his partners realized that buyers needed to be drawn to the area. Consequently, Beck built the Crescent Beach Hotel in 1914 and began his own cottage-building scheme. The hotel catered to those wanting peace and quiet and perhaps a good meal. Even with these enticements, Lakewood Park failed to thrive. Beck sold Lakewood Park and adjacent land in 1916 to his partners: F.A. Heldridge was the cashier at the Milford National Bank, C.B. Shay was a contractor who had done much work at Lakewood Park, and W.A. White was the proprietor of the Earling Hotel in Spencer. These men also formed the West Okoboji Country Club a year later.

THE CRESCENT HOUSE.

The 1914 Crescent House was well placed on the lake and was highly visible from passing steamboats. In addition to having access to a screened porch on the lower level, guests could find space on the second-floor veranda. Dormer windows on the roof provided flow-through ventilation for all. Situated on one of the main canals, the Crescent House was built with a naturalistic, rustic view in mind. Rusticating—briefly enjoying a peaceful time in a rough or rugged setting—continued to be somewhat fashionable through the 1920s. The bridge (shown below) next to the hotel qualifies as rustic due to its simplicity; the original was much more ornate and had a high arch. The windmill pumped the hotel's water until public water lines were installed.

THE BRIDGE AT THE CRESCENT HOUSE.

Gone are the romantic rustic bridges, and no gondola ever glided over Lakewood Park's canals. This aerial view may date from the 1930s, but it shows what the Crescent Beach Hotel (also called Crescent House, Crescent Lodge, or Crescent Inn) had to offer. A long dock accommodated steamboats as well as any pleasure boats, while the mostly unused canals sat idle. Note the cottages at right, which people began to prefer to rent over staying in hotels. William A. White's operation of the hotel beginning in 1916 saw it grow into a widely appreciated resort and dining establishment. His wife, Etta, continued to run the operation after he died in 1937. Etta summered at a cottage on the grounds until her death in 1954.

Crescent Beach Cottages on Okoboji Lake

Naper Photo

Crescent Beach had nearly 1,000 feet of lakeshore. Through the Depression and afterward, entrepreneurs found that small cottages were cheaper and easier to operate than a large hotel— even one that did not offer dancing or other expensive amenities. It was not long before cottages like these became commonplace around the lakes, and Crescent Beach began to fall in line. The Crescent Beach Hotel survived World War I, but during World War II, the shortages, rationing, and difficulty finding seasonal employees due to the war effort drastically diminished the number of reservations at the resort. In June 1943, Crescent House operator Etta White announced she would ride out the summer without opening. According to a classified ad, White offered the resort for sale in 1944. She did reopen it in 1944 but sold it in May 1945 to Carroll Lane of Carroll, Iowa.

Under Carroll Lane's ownership, the Crescent Beach resort flourished. In addition to putting up additional cabins, enlarging and refitting the 1914 hotel, and continuing to build along the lakeshore, Lane even made Crescent Beach into a convention destination. Meeting and dining spaces for groups were added, along with playgrounds and entertainment for children. In this mid-1950s image, one such group relaxes on one of the resort's docks.

The imposing visage of "Chief Okoboji," who greeted visitors in the lobby, was familiar to all who checked in at Crescent Beach. There was no Chief Okoboji, but gullible guests were often directed to the nearby Wahpeton high point to search for his grave. Fictional stories had been told about the chief for decades, making the wooden carving an indelible guest memory. Today, this figure still stands as the "Welcoming Chief" in the Crescent Beach Lodge lobby.

Amidst the wave of postwar optimism, the Crescent Beach resort became a major force in the 1950s and 1960s, with the property being enlarged or improved nearly every year. Rather than tear down the old lodge, owner Carroll Lane added on to it, constructing the modern and cleverly named Beach-O-Tel unit (above) next door. The new building had a large dining room, a waterfront private dining room, and an activity room on the upper level. Around this time, Crescent Beach's resort featured more than 100 units for families on vacation, and most enjoyed their own sand beach just steps from the front door. For children, the famous water wheel (below) provided endless hours of fun in West Okoboji. Today, in retrospect, some observe the water wheel as a potential death trap, but it certainly was fun at the time.

The 1,000 feet of Emerson Bay lakefront at Crescent Beach is shown in this postcard from the 1970s or early 1980s. At right, the 1914 Crescent Beach Resort lodge and 1955 Beach-O-Tel building give way to 14 cottages that extend all the way to the bridge and lagoon entrance. The Thunderbird lodge and guesthouse are at left, with the supper club immediately behind them. The resort was famous for its island playground, which still attracts children today. The resort changed hands around the time of this photograph and eventually passed to Dave Nodland and others. While those owners maintained the facilities shown here for some years, 540 feet of lakeshore were sold in 1991; everything to the right of the canal inlet was converted to individual homes. The once-expansive resort now exists only to the left of the inlet.

Seven

VACATION VILLAGE

One- or two-week family vacations became the norm in the second half of the 20th century as the "Greatest Generation" spawned baby boomers. Successful food broker Hobart Ross, who had owned the Manhattan Resort and converted it from a stodgy, timeworn hotel into a tidy cottage colony, envisioned a new, purpose-built location filled with similar cabins. Vacation Village opened in 1949 and offered not just 100 quaint, modern cabins to rent for one week or two but also a sand beach, swimming docks, rowboats and powerboats for rent, and planned activities for children—including the famous weekly "watermelon bust." The Ross family owned and managed Vacation Village until 1984. The area, now called Village West Resort and owned by Iowa Resort Holdings, LLC, was converted into a time-share resort with townhouses, apartments, and a 50-unit hotel. After the demise of the Inn in 2018, Village West could rightfully claim to be the largest resort on West Lake Okoboji, offering housing, restaurants, a marina with boat rentals, and even a convention facility. The sand beach remains a focal point for vacationers.

Businessman Hobart A. Ross, was the son of Iowa pioneers; his father, August, was a prominent merchant and banker in tiny Little Rock, Iowa. The family began vacationing at Okoboji in 1903, when Hobart was only six years old. In 1914, as a teenager, he found work in the grocery department of the A.M. Johnson Store in Spirit Lake, and the lessons he learned there must have stuck. He went on to found United Food Markets in 1923, introducing self-service shopping to Iowa homemakers. Just a decade later, after he had gained resort ownership experience in Florida, he purchased the Manhattan Resort. Ross foresaw cultural changes coming and envisioned a lakefront resort designed from the ground up with families in mind. The planning of Vacation Village began in October 1945. (Courtesy of the Ross family archives.)

In 1945, Hobart Ross purchased 68 acres of the Manley farm south of Egralharve for $15,000 and built this organized lakefront resort with 114 units. Ross sold his Manhattan Beach Cottages resort in 1948. Unlike traditional hotels, Vacation Village offered separate accommodations (each containing one to four bedrooms); a clubhouse; a grocery store; and a large hall used for dining, dances, conventions, movies, and children's activities. (Courtesy of the Ross family archives.)

A family resort should be run by a family, and Hobart Ross set up management of the enterprise for two of his sons, Keith and Bob Ross, who eventually purchased Vacation Village. News reports called it "the largest single summer resort project in the Lakes Region to be conceived by one man." In 1948, the Ross family opened the "village center" clubhouse. Fran Ross and her husband, Bob, are pictured here at the grand opening. (Courtesy of the Ross family archives.)

COME TO
Vacation Village

THE BIG VALUE IN FAMILY FUN VACATIONS!

From opening day, families were the focus at the Ross family's Vacation Village. This brochure depicting children having fun on the beach and in the water shows that they never strayed from that. Guests could rent rowboats and powerboats or ride on the *Queen* to the Arnolds Park amusement park. With no air-conditioning in the simple cabins, on hot nights, children often would sneak out to the beach and swim until one of the security guards caught them. The resort also published a weekly news sheet detailing the names and ages of guests. This proved to be a great way to spur childhood friendships. Vacation Village offered activity directors and babysitting but also organized competitive activities, talent shows, and even dances for both young and old.

For guests who returned annually throughout the 1950s and 1960s, the sight of this distinctive Vacation Village sign on Highway 86 could set hearts aflutter. The modern cottages had up-to-date amenities typical of the time: electric heat for cold days, refrigerators (not iceboxes) for food people could prepare themselves, and indoor plumbing—but no television, telephones, or even radio. Early news articles touted "such innovations as Venetian screens and plastic curtains" to suggest the resort's modernity. For most guests, especially children, planned recreational activities filled their days, making the cottage simply a place to sleep at night. Over the years, members of the Ross family received letters from adult guests who vacationed there as children thanking them for making memories that have lasted a lifetime. (Courtesy of the Ross family archives.)

Hobart Ross molded Vacation Village based on of other successful family resorts emerging at the time. He created a broad sand beach, along with docks, swimming areas, and 100 cottages that accommodated from 2 to 12 persons. Boat rentals were available for guests to take advantage of Okoboji's quality fishing, as the two people shown here are doing, or skiing. (Courtesy of the Ross family archives.)

Hobart Ross was initially criticized by the Iowa Department of Natural Resources when he was building Vacation Village due to unanticipated runoff, so he made drainage changes that permanently improved the stability of the lakefront. One involved the stabilization of the large sand beach he created. Some 60 years later, that beach is still used by guests, although bathing attire has changed somewhat since the 1950s.

A highlight of any Okoboji stay was a ride on an excursion boat like the *Queen* or the *Boji Belle* for a relaxing trip around the lake. The steamer *Queen* plied the waters of West Okoboji beginning in 1901. Moved to Okoboji in the late 1940s from Wayzata, Minnesota, the *Boji Belle* was originally a pleasure cruiser called the *Snark*. Around 1954, excursion line operator Bob Buhrow refitted the vessel with a riverboat motif and even added a dummy paddle wheel on the stern, renaming it the *Boji Belle*. He added the top-covering deck in 1958. It continued to serve the tourist trade until age took its toll. The *Boji Belle* was dry-docked at Maywood in the early 1960s and, in 1967, retired and moved ashore to the old Dickinson County Fairgrounds, where it functioned as a tourist information office until 1973. The Spirit Lake Chamber of Commerce sold the boat, and it was either dismantled or moved out of the area in 1976. (Courtesy of the Ross family archives.)

Children of all ages eagerly looked forward to the Vacation Village recreational activities, but for many, the sandcastle-building contest sparked keen competition. If one's creation was chosen as one of the winners, they could receive extravagant prizes, such as a candy bar from the resort's gift shop or the much-coveted plastic gold trophy. (Courtesy of the Ross family archives.)

At some point during a Vacation Village stay, the Village Hall was cleared and made into a dance floor. Dances were announced early in the week and featured local musicians and sometimes talented guests who would sit in. A Wurlitzer jukebox was available for tunes, too. Times have changed since the late 1950s, when ashtrays were common. (Courtesy of the Ross family archives.)

The resort regularly held "watermelon busts," which remain a prized vacation memory for many guests. Every week, the Rosses would bring in a pickup truck groaning under the weight of ripe watermelons, set up a carving table, and begin slicing the melons for guests to enjoy. As the above photograph shows, hungry children and their parents would swarm the serving table. Master melon-carver Carl Ross (wearing in a white shirt and located in the lower left corner of the image), son of operator Bob Ross, is shown preparing to add more watermelon to the serving table. In the image at right, two unidentified girls sporting stylish hats prepare to enjoy their pile of watermelon slices. Although these would not have been officially sanctioned, one can be sure there were seed-spitting contests taking place among the youth. These photographs date from the early 1960s. (Both, courtesy of the Ross family archives.)

Vacation Village also operated an early version of today's convenience shop, although at the time, it was probably viewed as a general store. Here, homemakers could find everyday staples like coffee, flour, eggs, cereals, and all the make-at-home foods they needed while staying in a cottage. When it first opened in 1949, the store had a straightforward selection of staples. Bottled Nehi soda pop and Coca-Cola were fast sellers. The clubhouse was remodeled in the 1960s with a gift shop that sold souvenirs in addition to offering candy, cigarettes, newspapers, and magazines. Employee May Kelly is shown dusting mementos in the below image, and the freezer in the foreground was stocked with plenty of frozen treats. (Both, courtesy of the Ross family archives.)

An impromptu waterskiing show was not out of the ordinary on a summer's day. Shown here around 1960, Martha Dalby (left) and a friend wave at the camera while skiing past Vacation Village's sand beach. Dalby was like many Vacation Village guests, coming to visit annually, and she became a friend of the Ross family. Vacation Village rented water skis and belts, along with boats. The resort rented wooden rowboats, made by Hafer Boatworks of Spirit Lake, through the 1950s. When fiberglass became available, the Ross family found boats made with the material were too heavy and somewhat uncomfortable to operate. They settled on simple aluminum fishing-type boats with outboard motors. The boathouse also sold minnows, worms, and other fishing equipment and, in later years, rented out personal watercraft and pontoon boats. (Courtesy of the Ross family archives.)

The Hotel Orleans, the Inn, Crandall's Lodge, and the early Manhattan Beach Resort all had open verandas or walkways where people could promenade to cool off during warm summer evenings. That old style of thinking was cast away for Vacation Village. Instead, each cottage had screened-in windows that allowed guests to stay inside—away from mosquitoes or other insects—and still catch a breeze. Cabins were also staggered so that no cabin totally blocked the view from any other one. This picture shows that some of the cabins had a view of the sand beach and West Okoboji from the screened porch. The resort was frequently praised by guests for the quality of its parklike landscaping and upkeep. In the distance is the boathouse, where boats and other recreational items could be rented. (Courtesy of the Ross family archives.)

The resort's spacious convention center afforded a location where group meetings could be held, but it also served as a dance hall, dining room, game room, billiard parlor, movie hall, and the only place on the grounds where one could watch television. A number of companies held annual meetings at Vacation Village each year, with the staff looking forward to seeing familiar faces each summer. Vacation Village advertised throughout the Midwest, and the resort continued to promote family vacations in Okoboji. By the 1960s, it was nearing the end of the baby boom generation that Hobart Ross foresaw, but catering to parents who were now in their 40s and 50s continued to pay off at Vacation Village. (Courtesy of the Ross family archives.)

The freedom that a rowboat can give a child is refreshing, and when they are on vacation at Okoboji, it is incalculable. Here, several families try their hands at navigating wooden rowboats away from the sand beach. Simple rowboats are now gone, having been replaced by personal watercraft, speedboats, pontoons, paddleboats, and kayaks for rent. Above the beach is the retaining wall that stabilized the beach, and beyond that, one can see the orderly—and breeze-catching—arrangement of cottages for guests. The current Village West Resort cottages are part of what is called Sunrise Cove. Most are modified A-frame buildings that range from studio to four-bedroom units. These are time-shares in which investors purchase a specific week for their exclusive use. Owners who choose not to use their rental during their specific week can have the resort rent it for that week, or they can trade weeks with other owners. (Courtesy of the Ross family archives.)

Eight

MOM-AND-POP RESORTS

Large resorts like the Inn were successful, but no vacation at Okoboji seemed complete without a stay at a small, informal mom-and-pop resort. While lakefront guest cottages began to dot the area by 1900, two eras in the history of Okoboji saw the proliferation of these resorts. The first was during the boom of the 1920s, when tiny, modern bungalows—with indoor plumbing and electricity—could be put up for just a few thousand dollars that could then be earned back in the first couple of summer seasons. The second boom occurred after World War II, when productivity soared, leisure time became more common, and veterans sought peace and tranquility at a lakefront resort. A typical mom-and-pop resort might have the owner and his wife living in a year-round home with anywhere from three to twelve tiny cottages for guests. Many baby boomers recall building childhood friendships with other young "lake rats" who vacationed at these resorts year after year. Kids could leave the cabin in the morning to spend an entire day on the lake with friends, perhaps hearing their parents admonish them to "be home when it gets dark." Ironically, Okoboji's popularity spelled an end to these as property values climbed and aging resort owners worried about a comfortable retirement. When one is in their late 60s and a developer offers them more money for their lakefront resort than they earned in a lifetime of hard work, it is not difficult to see how that offer would be hard to resist. The epitaphs of these small businesses were soon written in real estate "for sale" advertisements.

Longtime boatbuilder Cecil Nelson's West Side Boat Livery had blossomed into a cabin resort when Ray Worden and his wife purchased it in the early 1960s. This view shows a typical Spirit Lake day and looks south down the dock toward the cabins and office. Note the Hafer rowboats on the right and the vintage auto in the drive. This later became Vergie's Southside Resort. (Courtesy of Sally Ann Scheib.)

Whether one is fishing from a boat or from the long dock, actually catching something is an exciting vacation event worthy of documenting on film. Here, the Scheib family—(from left to right) Steve, Susan, Margaret, and Sally—from Cedar Rapids, Iowa poses with their catch. (Courtesy of Sally Ann Scheib.)

Established in the 1910s by C.H. Harlan, the resort bearing his name on Big Spirit's northeast side was a favored fishing destination. Fishing cabins and amenities were added over time. This photograph from 1964 shows the simple pleasures to be had when Harlan Beach owners Bud and Margaret Gregersen operated the resort. The resort got new owners again in 1997, and they eventually focused on mobile home living rather than cabins. (Courtesy of Rob Gregersen.)

The Harlan family's original cottages no doubt attracted fishermen, and by the 1940s, Harland Beach had a new owner—H.C. Beard. In this 1947 newspaper ad, he touts his 10 new cottages with hot and cold showers for visitor comfort. The addition of 10 boats also surely contributed to the amenities that discerning guests wanted at that time.

For years, Herman "Slim" Mason was Big Spirit Lake's unofficial mayor. An avid outdoorsman, Mason could be counted on to provide both tourists and locals with an accurate accounting of fishing and hunting quality on the waters. His North Shore Cabins were typical of small resorts: a few modest buildings with fast access to the water. Amenities—other than fishing tackle and bait—were few. Mason (right) is shown above in the 1940s with rural mail carrier Lee W. Smith of Spirit Lake, and the two likely spent hours observing life. By the time Mason established his resort, many of the older resorts on the north shore were already gone. The 1950 newspaper map below shows the location of "Slim Mason's Resort." All of Mason's cabins have been razed or significantly renovated over the years. (Above, courtesy of Mary Bjorenson Dreier.)

Ruth and Norman Larson built this tidy resort colony, located directly east of Templar Park on the east side of Big Spirit in Orleans, after buying the main house from game warden Gus Meier in 1948. They operated Larson's Modern Cottages for more than 20 years. Fishermen especially appreciated the 20 units and 20 aluminum fishing boats available. As was common at most resorts, the Larsons also sold bait and tackle.

Beginning in 1946, Franklin Fedderson and his wife, Georgia, operated the Log Cabin Resort on Angler's Bay at Big Spirit Lake, which was easily identifiable from the water due to its large stone walls. The resort had 268 feet of sand beach, 11 units, and an actual log cabin built in 1918. In 1972, the Feddersons sold the resort to Merle Baker, who ran it until it closed in 1976.

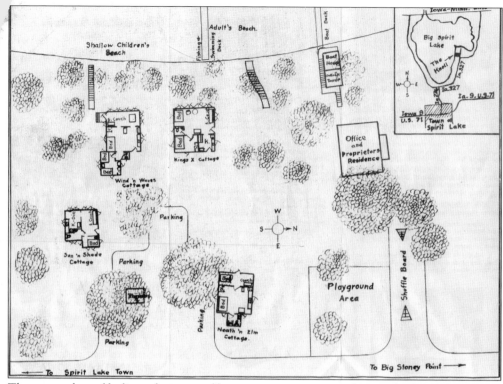

The extent that self-reliant, do-it-yourself resort owners go to is evident in this hand-drawn map outlining all that The Knoll resort offered on Spirit Lake. Unflagging hosts and schoolteachers L. Clark Close and his wife, Irene, started the business in July 1930 with the four cottages shown here. The Closes shut down the resort in 1973.

A mom-and-pop resort probably does not get much cuter than McBurney's Cottage Resort in Spirit Lake. It was located just north of Gilbert Park on East Okoboji. The resort was only around through the 1940s, when it became the Doran Cottages. Glenn and Leone Doran sold the 12-unit resort to Lester Freeman in 1951. Amazingly, a few of these adorable little cabins still stand today.

BROOKS BEACH E. OKOBOJI LAKE 6524

Although few people remember Sioux City Beach on East Okoboji, they can no doubt identify Brooks Beach. The Brooks Resort on East Okoboji was started around 1920 by Melford Brooks and was operated for many years by his son, Val Brooks, who also built Brooks National Golf Course across Highway 71, and then Melford's grandson Bud Brooks. At one time, guests could play on a miniature golf course built in 1935. The below image shows how close the cabins were to the railroad, but homemade stone-and-cement "yard art" made the resort easily identifiable to vacationers arriving from the highway. The Brooks Beach cabins still stand but are now individually owned and governed by a homeowners' association.

DRIVE WAY AT SIOUX CITY BEACH

COTTAGES AT GATESWOOD   ARNOLDS PARK, IOWA   E-200

The Gateswood Cottage colony on Highway 71 in Arnolds Park was billed as "a particular place for particular people." The Gateswood Cottages were developed by Olus Gates and operated by the Gates and Gardner families for years. The resort, known for its extravagant landscaping and secure environment (the Gates family hired private security), became part of the Fillenwarth Beach complex in 1978.

As society loosened, the Iowa Great Lakes became a girls' weekend destination, and the six friends shown here enjoyed a visit at Gateswood in 1955. From left to right, they are Georgia Brower, Pat Foley, Madonna Dries, Doris Wills, Shirley Dries, and Karroll Peterson, all from Sibley, Iowa. Even though there were also young men staying at the resort, the weekend was reported to be entirely innocent. (Courtesy of Madonna Dries Christensen.)

To be in the heart of the action in Arnolds Park in the 1940s, one could not beat staying at Turnley's Cottages, which were located in between the Central Ballroom and the Roof Garden. Run by Howard Turnley (who operated both dancing establishments) and his wife, Muriel, who owned the Peacock Restaurant, the 36 cottages were made from lumber salvaged from the old Arnolds Park Hotel that was dismantled in 1939.

The Lincoln Park Resort was built in 1899 by Margaret "Grandma" Brosius, a woman the *Milford Mail* reported to be "happy and jolly and [who] easily made friends," which made her place "very popular with summer vacationists." After Brosius sold the resort in 1919, ownership changed hands several times in nearly every decade. Located just west of the Arnolds Park amusement park, the resort house survived two tornadoes but was burned in 1985 as part of firefighter training.

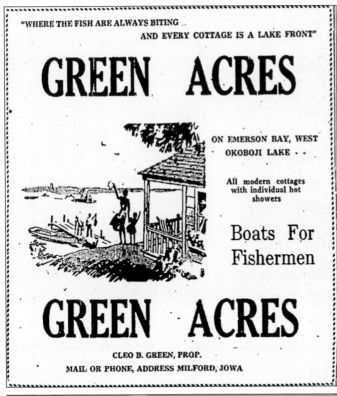

"WHERE THE FISH ARE ALWAYS BITING ..
AND EVERY COTTAGE IS A LAKE FRONT"

GREEN ACRES

ON EMERSON BAY, WEST
OKOBOJI LAKE · ·

All modern cottages
with individual hot
showers

Boats For
Fishermen

GREEN · ACRES

CLEO B. GREEN, PROP.
MAIL OR PHONE, ADDRESS MILFORD, IOWA

In 1939, Spencer newspaper publisher Dent Green purchased 82 acres on Emerson Bay with plans to build 30 cottages, improve the property with massive tree plantings, and possibly erect a ski jump and bobsled track. Only the cottages and plantings came to fruition. Dent's wife, Cleo, operated the resort during World War II and continued for 30 years afterward. This location is now home to the Emerson Bay Recreation Area and the Lighthouse Point condominium complex.

Overlooking Breezy Point in Emerson Bay, the Holiday Villa was started in 1962 by Dr. Ivan E. Brown of Hartley, Iowa. After being forced to turn down guest requests for two years, the Browns added a second building of eight units. The resort became a condominium complex that still bears the same name today. (Courtesy of Joan Brown.)

During the 1940s, Don Daily and his wife, Mildred, put up some casual cottages in Millers Bay to complement their boat livery business. Otto "Spud" Peterson was a service station operator from Spencer who longed for a peaceful fishing location. He bought Daily's Resort in 1958, giving the resort his distinctive nickname, and operated it with his wife, Harriette. The Dailys kept one of the cottages for themselves and enjoyed watching Spud build his own resort business. When Spud retired in 1971, new owners Dick and Kay Schmitt kept the name; it would just be easier, they reported. Spud's Resort, with its nine cabins, continued to be an area landmark until it was sold in 1991. Developer Ned Lenox remodeled the cabins and created a colony he called the Painted Ladies Retreat. The cabins eventually passed into individual private ownership, and a few still stand today in all their Victorian glory.

Started in 1937 by Spencer businessman John B. Flindt, Camp Hiawatha consisted of four cottages on Hiawatha Point at Miller's Bay. By 1940, Flindt had added a fourplex, offering "the finest accommodations in the middle west" and promising new guests their money back if it did not meet their expectations. Flindt sold the resort in 1945 to Ed Calhoun, who died unexpectedly two years later at age 50. Subsequent owners included Don and Tilly Smith, Chick Homan, and Ed Kelly. With more than 200 feet of shoreline on a high rise, Camp Hiawatha and its six cottages offered views of the length of West Okoboji. The property was sold for development in 1986. (Both, courtesy of Walt Homan.)

Sac City, Iowa, businessman Gerk Jansen came to town and bought Raebel's Resort on Estherville Beach on West Okoboji in 1945—only three months after Bob and Esther Raebel were attacked by a former employee and Bob was killed. Gregarious and entrepreneurial, Jansen followed the Raebels' successful pattern of offering a full recreational experience for the entire family. With a lot of vacant farmland behind the 800 feet of shoreline, Gerk's Resort was, for a time, the only place to offer horseback riding in addition to lake activities. Gerk's grew to have 34 cottages and 56 camping units for trailers. In 1973, Jansen sold the resort. Those buyers sold to Nodland Investment Corporation, which used the land to create the Landings housing development in 1990. Gerk's daughter Vergie Jansen Hill went on to own Vergie's Southside Resort on Spirit Lake.

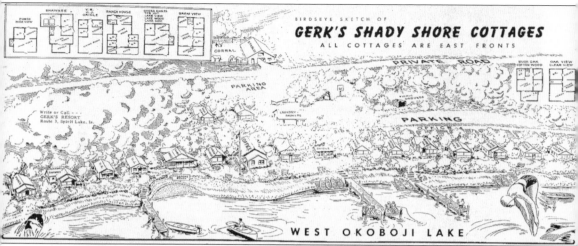

This tourism magazine advertisement for Gerk's Shady Shore Cottages (the name did not stick, as it became, simply, Gerk's Resort) shows the expanse of Estherville Beach at the time. In the early days, Gerk's had only 17 cottages and camping spaces for tents and trailers. Amenities included a shower facility and a large picnic area. A grocery store was constructed. A playground area was added for children, as well as supervised beach and swimming activities. Even today, people who vacationed at Gerk's as children recall the playground equipment, especially the trampolines installed in the 1960s. As trailers and motor homes became more common, Gerk's began offering seasonal leases.

Clements Cottages
Okoboji Lake

Clements Beach, carved out of south Manhattan Beach, came to be almost by accident. Drs. Walter and Jean Mendenhall bought lots from Joseph I. Myerly in 1907 after vacationing here for two years. Jean's father, William H. Clements, visited and bought an adjacent lot in 1913. Clements was a carpenter, and he erected a vacation home that quickly became a social center largely thanks to his wife, Jessie. Guests arrived, and more cottages were added over the years. After William Clements died in 1925, and Jessie in 1933, operation passed to Jean Mendenhall, then to Jean's son Wally and his wife, Alice, both of whom gave up their teaching careers to run things full-time in 1947. The resort was sold in 1977.

Naper Photo
Play Ground At Clements Cottages

Luther Babcock, from Spencer, clerked at the Inn, the Arnolds Park Hotel, and finally, the Manhattan Beach hotel as a manager and real estate salesman. The commission from his early sales earned him enough to buy three south Manhattan lots, and in 1913, he built his first vacation cottage. Sixteen more followed over the years. This postcard view dates from the late 1950s.

Children staying at Babcock's often developed summer friends from nearby resorts. For decades, there was a nearly unbroken run of resort cottages from Clement's to Babcock's and up to the Myerly Cottages and Manhattan Beach. While these comfortable cottages provided parents with lake views and cool breezes, nothing beat a summertime of lakefront fun for kids. This photograph is likely from the 1940s.

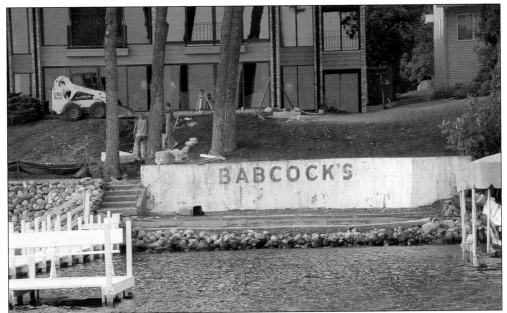

Luther C. Babcock died in 1955, and his widow, Alice, ran the resort until she sold it to Rodney Parsons in 1964. The 200 feet of lakeshore and 12 remaining cottages were then sold in 1970. The family resort, which had been continually operated since 1913, passed into history the next year, when a condominium complex was erected on the site. This photograph shows both the old and new Colony Condominiums.

When one's family owns a resort, they plan for part of their summertime weekends to involve cleaning cottages, and thus it was for the Jensen family in the 1970s. Informally begun by Jack and Annette Neighbor in the 1950s, Jensen's Sunset Beach resort added these cottages in the 1960s. Operation passed to the Neighbors' children, the Jensens, who moved to season-long cottage rentals only and eventually closed the resort around 1992.

This view of the doughnut-shaped Lazy Lagoon Resort—with an island in the middle—is from around 1950, but its origin was actually in 1928. Alex W. Percival, who operated the Northwood Tourist Park on his farmland on West Okoboji's north end, struck a partnership with the *Sioux City Tribune* to develop 178 lakefront acres. Roads and this unique circular lagoon were installed as part of the Triboji development.

Likely built by the Weed family—Frank Weed and his son Judd bought or built as many as 35 cottages over the years—in the 1950s, the group of cabins on Spirit Lake across from the fish hatchery seemingly changed hands every couple of years. Owner Darrel Wilkinson sold to John Winbauer, who sold to sale barn owner Harold Ohlson. In 1960, Bob and Dee Olson of Alta, Iowa, purchased Ohlson's Cottonwood Cottages in Orleans, running the resort's nine cottages for more than 25 years. While it was hard work growing up at a resort where kids were expected to help out at all times, it could also produce fun. Pictured in 1963 are, from left to right, Cindy and George Gross, Olson cousin Gregg Sunner, Bob and Dee's daughters Jolene and Marsha Olson, and Olson cousin Scott Sunner.

East Okoboji's Lakeview Beach, where the Ritz bar and grill is now located, was first home to Charles and Alma Wilson, who operated a livery and guide service and Lakeview Beach Resort. In 1944, they sold to Ralph Gregerson, with Charles acting as a fishing guide until 1947. After it was renamed Gregerson's Resort, the new owner added amenities and units—up to 21 units, as shown in the c. 1958 photograph above. Ralph's son Don Gregerson and his wife, Marge, ran the resort until they sold it in 1966, when the property became Grand Vue Beach Resort. Later owners Dave and Linda Mitchell added lakeshore dining with the Dock & Dine Restaurant. One of the Gregerson buildings is part of the present-day Ritz, which opened in 1989. Below, a young Don Gregerson takes a brief rest on one of the resort's many wooden rowboats in the 1940s. (Both, courtesy of Don Gregerson.)

Name	MAP NO.	GRID	Name	MAP NO.	GRID
ALLEN KECK COTGS.	1	F20	LAKESHORE MOTEL	74	G17
ANGLERS' BAY RES.	2	N1	LAKES LANES BOWLING	75	H12
ARNOLD'S AMUS. PK.	3	F19	LAKE VU MOBIL RES.	76	G17
BAY-RYM CONDMS.	4	C13	LARSON'S COTGS.	77	L15
BENIT COTGS.	5	F19	LARSON'S RES.	78	K6
BENSON COTGS.	6	F20	LEE'S RESORT	79	C11
BIG STONEY RES.	7	L4	LIGHTHOUSE CONDM.	80	B20
BLUE BIRD ROCK	8	G18	LINCOLN PARK RES.	81	F19
BLUE WATER BCH. RE.	9	C11	LUTHERAN BIBLE CMP.	82	C18
BOAT HAVEN MARINE	10	G19	MANHATTAN BCH. RES.	83	C16
BOJI BELLE INFO	11	H11	MASSACRE MONUMENT	84	F19
BROOKS BCH. CTGS.	12	G17	MAVERICK RESTAURANT	85	B18
BROWN'S COTGS.	13	F19	MAX SEELY RESORT	86	L14
CASS BAY COTGS.	14	G18	MCKINNEY COTGS.	87	H18
CEN LA CAMP GRDS.	15	G13	MIDWAY DRIVE-IN	88	I9
CENTER L. BOAT LIV.	16	F13	MILLER BAY STORE	89	B18
CENTER LAKE VILL.	17	G12	MITCHELL'S CTGS.	90	L14
CENTRAL EMPORIUM	18	G19	NAVAJO COTGS.	91	F19
CHATEAU CONDMS.	19	G18	NEW INN, THE	92	E16
CHELSEA CONDMS.	20	B18	NORTH BAY CONDMS.	93	C11
CLEMENT'S BCH. CTGS.	21	C17	OAK BAY COTGS.	94	B17
COLONY CONDMS.	22	C16	OAK HILL CAFE, CTGS.	95	G19
CONNER'S COURT	23	F20	OAKS MOTEL	96	K11
COOL CREST RES.	24	K7	OAKS, THE, COTGS.	97	I8
COTTONWOOD CTGS.	25	J8	O'FARRELL SIS. REST.	98	G18
COUNTRY CLUB VILLAS	26	F16	OKOBOJI BOATS	99	G18
COWAN'S COTGS.	27	I9	OKOB. BOATS WAREH'S.	100	H19
CRESCENT BCH. RES.	28	C19	OKOBOJI MOTEL	101	G17
DANBOM MARINE	29	E22	ORLEANS PARK	102	J8
DANBOM RESORT	30	D21	ORLEANS SWIM. BCH.	103	J8
DECKS COURT RES.	31	F19	PARKVIEW MOTEL	104	F19
EDGEWATER PLAZA	32	G17	PASTIME COTGS.	105	I9
ELLSWORTH COTGS.	33	D21	PEACOCK LOUNGE	106	G19
ENGLISH'S COTGS.	34	C18	PECK'S BOAT LIV.	107	K15
FILLENWARTH BCH.	35	G19	PICK'S COTGS.	108	F19
FISHERMAN'S WHARF	36	G18	PRESSEL'S COTGS.	109	F19
FOUR SEASONS RES.	37	G18	RAINBOW RESORT	110	K8
FOXIE'S RESORT	38	F19	RED ROOSTER CAFE	111	G18
FREEMANS COTGS.	39	I10	REED'S RUN RESORT	112	K6
FUNLAND & CHAR HS.	40	I9	ROG'S TACKLE SHOP	113	G18
GARDNER CABIN	41	F19	ROOF GARDEN	114	F19
GATESWOOD CTGS.	42	G19	ROYAL COURT CTGS.	115	H19
GEE'S COTGS.	43	F19	RUDY'S BANANA	116	G18
GERK'S RESORT	44	B12	SANDBAR BCH. RES.	117	N3
GIBSON SPORT.GDS.	45	J16	SANDPIPER COVE CDMS.	118	B12
GILBERT PARK	46	J10	SANFORD'S COTGS.	119	E21
GINGHAM INN	47	I18	SHADY LANE CTGS.	120	K8
GRANDVIEW BCH.	48	H18	SHADY REST RES.	121	H18
GRANDVUE CTGS.	49	L15	SHAMROCK MOTEL	122	H12
HACKETT'S RES.	50	F19	SHUCK'S BAIT STORE	123	B22
HALE'S BCH. CTGS.	51	I8	SIMMONS SUNSET SHR.	124	K5
HARLAN BCH. RES.	52	N2	SMITH TRAILER CRT.	125	G18
HEATHER RIDGE CND.	53	B20	SMOKEY'S STK HS ✱	126	E22
HEDGE-ROW CTGS.	54	C11	SOUTH SIDE RES.	127	I8
HESS COTGS.	55	G18	SPORTSMAN'S OF A.P.	128	G19
HI HO CLUB	56	F19	SPUD'S RESORT	129	B18
HILLTOP HOUSE	57	H12	STONER'S CTGS.	130	D21
HI POINT CLUB	58	A17	TACO HOUSE	131	F20
HOLIDAY INN MOTEL	59	G16	TEEG'S STEAK HS.	132	E22
HOLIDAY VILLA RES.	60	B20	TREASURE VILL. THEA.	133	A21
HUT, THE	61	G19	TRIGG'S LAKESH. MO.	134	H18
IDSO INN	62	G19	TWEETER'S OKOB. LNG.	135	G17
INN BETWEEN MO.	63	G17	VACATION VILLAGE	136	C14
JEFF & MABEL'S GROC.	64	J8	VERN & COILA'S REST.	137	D21
JENSEN'S S.BCH. CTGS.	65	F19	VILLA, THE, RESORT	138	G18
JEPSEN'S RES.	66	I9	WATERS EDGE APTS.	139	G19
JESS & CONNIE'S GRO.	67	B18	WHITE OAKS CAMP	140	F20
JULIUS COTGS.	68	F19	WHITE OAKS STORE	141	F20
KABELE'S TRAD. POST	69	I9	WILSON BOAT WKS.	142	G18
KINGWOOD CTGS.	70	H18	WINAKAWIN, CAMP	143	H19
KURIO KASTLE	71	G18	WOODLEY MOBIL CRT.	144	H21
LAKES ART CENTER	72	G17	YACHT CLUB	145	E16
LAKES CENTER MALL (AREA CHAM. OF COMM.)	73	G19	✱ NOW KEITH & HAROLD'S OASIS.	126	E22

This glossary, dated 1976, details many of the resorts, restaurants, bars, and places for fun at Okoboji. Many resorts listed here have passed into history: Allen-Keck, Benit, Benson, Big Stoney Resort, Cowans, Hales Beach, Kingswood, Max Seely Resort, Oak Bay Cottages, Rainbow Resort, Reed's Run, Sanford's, along with others not listed. There is no doubt that all of them still hold a place in Okoboji vacationers' hearts.

Nine

TODAY'S
LAKEFRONT SURVIVORS

With so many traditional lakefront resorts now just a memory, conventional wisdom suggests the Iowa Great Lakes will become private—for the privileged only. Thanks to determination, planning, luck, and business acumen, a handful of traditional lakefront resorts remain at which families can book a summertime visit without having to buy a time-share or engage in other schemes. New competing vacation innovations include condominiums and patio homes for rent that can be booked online with virtually no face-to-face interaction and no social amenities on offer. West Okoboji resorts can be counted on one hand: Crescent Beach, Four Seasons, Pick's, Hedge-Row, and Fillenwarth Beach. East Okoboji has the relatively new Bridges Bay hotel, but it is overshadowed by the development's own condominiums and patio homes. Remaining on East Okoboji are the Triggs Bay and Pioneer Beach resorts, although the latter will likely soon move to season-long rentals only. A single traditional lakefront operation remains on Big Spirit Lake at Sand Bar Beach. Many of these survivors are owned by people at or nearing retirement age, which calls the fate of these resorts into question. For now, however, residents and visitors alike can enjoy them and thank the owners for maintaining a cherished Okoboji tradition.

Located on East Okoboji, Kruse's Beach's 10 simple cabins offered just the basics for an Okoboji stay. The resort was bought in the 1940s by Richard and Helen James, who created Jimmy's Cottages and Jimmy's Boat Livery. Chester Triggs bought the cabins in 1950 and operated Triggs Resort with his family for decades.

Run since 1980 by Mike May and his wife, Marge (Chester Triggs's daughter), Triggs Bay Resort sees many guests rebooking at the end of their stay to return year after year. A far cry from the simple cabins originally named after US presidents, the modern resort boasts 250 feet of sand beach, a heated swimming pool, and 46 condominium-style units.

West Okoboji's Crescent Beach is discussed elsewhere in this book, but its many cabins and motel-style buildings have been considerably reduced. The resort now offers 29 rooms and suites, four condominiums, and the Grand Lodge—the former Crescent Beach Restaurant. With its sandy beach and playground island that was created as part of the Lakewood Park development, it continues to draw visitors to Emerson Bay.

Pioneer Beach grew out of farmland on East Okoboji's east side in 1920 but was slow to develop. In 1954, Anne and Wilbur Steen started Pioneer Beach Resort and boat livery with five cabins. Over the decades, a series of avid fishermen owned the resort, making a few changes. Today, Rick and Lisa Vander Woude, who opened a popular outdoor bar, are exploring seasonal-only rentals for their eight units.

A few of the 1920s- and 1930s-era cottages erected near the grade by Harry and Dorothy Hart became B&B Cottages when Betty and Bert Nystrom bought them in the 1950s. This 1970s photograph shows a few remaining cottages along the waterfront, although these were soon replaced. The new hotel building at left was erected by Harvey DeVries in 1965 as part of Water's Edge Resort.

After the Four Seasons resort was bought by Dean Mitchell and family in 1969, expansion and development continued for years. "People don't want the old cottages anymore—they want the air-conditioning, shag carpet and television," Mitchell said in 1978. Today, an RV and camping area is gone, along with Hart's cottages, replaced by more modern motel-style lakefront accommodation and the Dry Dock Lounge, added in 1981. The restaurant and resort are both open during all four seasons.

The Four Seasons resort has both lakefront and off-lake units, all built in a modern motel style—but the shag rugs are gone. The Dry Dock Lounge, shown here at the left edge of the picture, continues to be popular with both vacationers and locals. It offers summertime outdoor seating and affords an unobstructed view of the Smith's Bay boat traffic.

Pillsbury Point's summer camping grounds eventually evolved into seasonal cabins. After this area was developed in 1900 by Robert Schofield of Colorado with 10 cottages and a larger home, Al Harges of Sheldon bought Schofield's Pillsbury Point land in 1916. The Harges family then operated a lively fishing and resort business for 27 years. Gregor and Theresa Pick bought the Harges' resort in 1944. (Courtesy of Jensen Real Estate.)

Charging $3 per night in the early days, Pick's Resort—with cottages painted a signature cheery yellow—was easily visible from boats. Pick's Resort grew to include more than a dozen on- and off-lake buildings, with Theresa Pick running things well past her 100th birthday. In 2013, the valuable lakefront property was sold to a private homeowner, but the mostly off-lake cottages remain. (Courtesy of Jensen Real Estate.)

In 1918, A.T. Fillenwarth of Sanborn, Iowa, put up a no-frills fishing cottage—it did not even have windows—on some land he owned in Arnolds Park, naming the cottage "Old Faithfull." Not long after this, a man offered to rent Old Faithfull for the week. When several more offers followed, A.T. and Sadie Fillenwarth, shown here in 1943, decided to erect more buildings. (Courtesy of Fillenwarth Beach.)

By the early 1920s, A.T. Fillenwarth had built seven cottages, all with glass windows. This was followed by 12 more on the lake bank. By 1930, he had 36 cottages, all with modern conveniences such as toilets, although "air conditioned by God," as A.T. stated. In this photograph, two unidentified women point out the modern attributes advertised on the resort's welcoming billboard. (Courtesy of Fillenwarth Beach.)

A.T. Fillenwarth's son Kenneth became involved as a teenager, building docks, making repairs, and giving boat rides. He continued to operate the resort with his family—daughters Lynn and Julie—following A.T.'s death in 1971. This lovely lakefront walkway view was destroyed in a 1968 tornado and replaced with a modern motel-style building. (Courtesy of Fillenwarth Beach.)

Fillenwarth Beach saw substantial growth through the 1970s. The current Fillenwarth South Beach (next to the Arnolds Park beach) came to be in 1974 with the purchase of the former Parkview Motel. The Cottage Colony was added in 1978 by acquiring the Gateswood Resort. Also during this time, Old Faithfull was converted into the indoor pool building. Fillenwarth Beach can now rightfully claim to be the largest traditional lakefront resort operating on West Okoboji, as it continues to offer old-style amenities for guests, like lake excursions on the resort's own tour boats, social events, children's activities, indoor and outdoor swimming, and even sailing and history cruises. After the deaths of Kenneth Fillenwarth, in 2014, and his daughter Julie, in 2017, Kenneth's daughter Lynn now runs the resort with a dedicated staff. She reports that there are plans in place to keep the resort going for new generations. (Courtesy of Fillenwarth Beach.)

Pioneer W.G. Jenkins's 1878 trapping, fishing, and boat livery business at Big Spirit's Sand Bar Bridge was a sportsman's retreat. Contractor, outdoorsman, farmer, and adventurer Lon Main bought the Jenkins boat business in 1913. It passed into the hands of brothers Pete and Sam Omer a decade later. This photograph of the resort's numerous fishing boats likely dates from the 1940s.

Lon Main turned the Sand Bar Resort into a complete fishing business, and in 1923, he sold it to the Omer brothers, Pete and Sam. News articles stated that the Omers "have popularized the lunch counter" for patrons. "Shore lunches" were a staple for hungry Sand Bar fishing guests. Some Omer relatives are shown visiting in the 1930s. The building behind them is still used today, with its counter stools remaining intact.

Today, the Sandbar Beach resort is a collection of 15 cabins, some of which were brought across the ice from Baker's Point resort in the late 1970s. Now featuring fully modern cabins, the resort was operated by the late Don Yarnes until his death in 2008. Don's grandfather Consider A. "Sid" Yarnes established much of the farmland surrounding the place. Don's widow, Nancy, now maintains the resort. It remains a favorite with anglers.

An unidentified girl amuses herself at the beach in 2018. The Sandbar Beach resort is actually built on a sandbar. High-water years have all but obliterated this feature, but it returns in subsequent drought seasons. This view shows the shoreline curve that, years ago, would have revealed other resorts in the distance, including Harlan Beach.

In this photograph that includes the iconic Sandbar Beach neon sign at right, the lunch counter (now an office) is shown with some of the cabins believed to have originally come from Baker's Point. Eagle-eyed readers will note that the sign is anchored to a tree. In the early days, the resort provided many wooden rowboats for anglers. Today, visitors often bring their own kayaks for recreation.

This sunset view of the fishing dock at Sandbar Beach Resort shows fishermen enjoying peace and quiet as it envelops Big Spirit Lake. Sandbar Beach has, since its inception, been a place of solitude where anglers can pit their wits and fishing tackle against fish while onshore families gather to enjoy simpler activities. In many ways, this resort is a throwback to a vacation one's grandparents might have taken: fishing, cooking the catch over a grill or open fire, al fresco dining with the setting sun, and maybe a cold beverage from the refrigerator, followed by retiring at darkness. Bait and a few staples are available at the office. Sandbar Beach has managed to survive by integrating annual mobile home leases into the business, which provides regular income—these lots are located at either end of the resort property. Resorts around the lakes without these types of property assets have disappeared. Countless families have spent quality recreation time on the Iowa Great Lakes, but today, locations where a family can rent a simple lakefront cabin are few and far between.

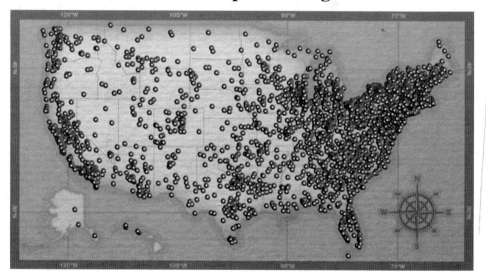